THE REALITIES OF TEACHING HISTORY:
BEGINNINGS

The Realities
of Teaching History:
Beginnings

Edited by
WILLIAM LAMONT

Published by
CHATTO & WINDUS
for
SUSSEX UNIVERSITY PRESS

1972

Published by
Chatto & Windus for
Sussex University Press

*

Clarke, Irwin & Co Ltd
Toronto

ISBN 0 85621 009 9

© William Lamont 1972

Printed in Great Britain by
T. & A. Constable Ltd
Hopetoun Street
Edinburgh 7

CONTENTS

'The other day I had occasion to write something about the teaching of history in private schools, and the following scene, which was only rather loosely connected with what I was writing, floated into my memory. It was less than fifteen years ago that I witnessed it.

'"Jones!"

'"Yessir!"

'"Causes of the French Revolution?"

'"Please, sir, the French Revolution was due to three causes, the teachings of Voltaire and Rousseau, the oppression of the nobles by the people and—". At this moment a faint chill, like the first premonitory symptom of an illness, falls upon Jones. Is it possible that he has gone wrong somewhere? The master's face is inscrutable. Swiftly Jones casts his mind back to the unappetising little book, with the gritty brown cover, a page of which is memorized daily. He could have sworn he had the whole thing right. But at this moment Jones discovers for the first time the deceptiveness of visual memory. The whole page is clear in his mind, the shape of every paragraph accurately recorded, but the trouble is that there is no saying which way round the words go. He had made sure it was the oppression of the nobles by the people; but then it might have been the oppression of the people by the nobles. It is a toss-up. Desperately he takes his decision—better to stick to his first version. He gabbles on: "The oppression of the nobles by the people and—"

'"Jones!"

'Is that kind of thing still going on, I wonder?'

GEORGE ORWELL, 14th March 1947

The above extract from *Tribune* reprinted in George Orwell, *Collected Essays, Journalism and Letters*, edited by S. Orwell and I. Angus (Secker and Warburg, 1968) is reproduced by kind permission of A. M. Heath and Co. Ltd on behalf of the Orwell Estate.

INTRODUCTION

WE have many handbooks on how to teach history. We have grander—and sometimes less helpful—books on the philosophy of history teaching. What we often lack is insight into the problems that face the young student when he attempts, during his first couple of years as a teacher, to translate theory into practice. This is perhaps the period when we lose many of our history teachers. Informally this was brought home to me with force by private letters from past students. They record—often movingly—the anguish and occasionally the euphoria of this crucial period.

This book grew out of these experiences. I asked three of my former students to keep a frank record of their experiences as beginners. Their story is told in the second section of the book. It is neither a success story nor a chase after gimmicks, but a truthful account of the ups-and-downs involved in putting the principles they believed in into practice during their first years of teaching.

What did the three students have in common? They cared for their subject: they cared for their children. But they were not supermen; absolutely essential for the purpose of this book, *they were not the sort of people to pretend that they were.* This book rests on their integrity. Second, they had all worked at Thomas Bennett Comprehensive School under the supervision of John Townsend, the Head of the Department of History. Not at the same time, however: Pat Kendell and Carlos Hood obtained their Post-Graduate Certificate of Education from the University of Sussex in the summer of 1968; Chris Culpin obtained his a year later. The method of training by which Pat, Carlos and Chris learned their craft alongside a skilled, practising teacher is unusual enough to deserve a chapter in itself. That is why, in the first section of the book, John Townsend explains at some length how the beginners themselves began. But I would like to insert a brief comment here. The conventional form of teacher-training, in which students deliver demonstration lessons before a University tutor twice a term, has a desperately histrionic air about it. My own experience on such a course must be a common one. Before a very difficult class I had given a wonderful lesson on Mary, Queen of Scots. My tutor departed smilingly ten minutes from the end, only because there is a limit to the amount of brilliance that any human being can be exposed to for any length of time. And as the door shut— and I was exulting in my powers—a voice at the front said: 'Are you glad we behaved ourselves today, sir?'

The Sussex experiment was an attempt to slay this cant. A pair of students were placed for the whole year in the same school for three days a week under the direct supervision of a practising teacher. The students were not 'marked' by the teacher: there were, fortunately, no grades attached to the Sussex Certificate. But at the end of each term the teacher/tutor wrote a full report on the progress of his students: this was seen by them, and discussed with them, before being sent to the University. In the final analysis the assessment of the students' competence to teach was entirely in the hands of their teacher/tutor.

I say 'the Sussex experiment' and, at once, replace one form of cant by another. In two ways the term misleads. I make it sound unique to Sussex, which it is not. York, Leicester and Cambridge are three names which instantly come to mind as areas experiment-ing along lines not dissimilar from our own. Also I make it sound new, which it is not. Mrs Frances Lawrence, who contributes the chapter on textbooks in the third section of this book, discovered recently in her researches an astonishingly perceptive pamphlet, written as early as 1904 by a Professor Adamson under the title, *Our Defective System of Training Teachers*. He argued for reform:

'For example, the German *Seminar*, established by Prussia so long ago as 1890, affords one possible model for imitation. The following summary, by a recent observer, indicates the manner of its employment, and at the same time very well illustrates what is to be understood by the phrase 'a real technical training for teachers'. The Seminar is attached to a well-staffed and well-equipped secondary school especially chosen for the purpose; the headmaster is professor of peda-gogy *ad hoc*, an experienced colleague assisting him as Master of Method, and both being paid an *honorarium* by the State. Here a group of four, six or eight students, after completing their University studies, assemble for a year's training. 'They hear and themselves draw up pedagogic reports, summaries of books or articles treating questions of innovation or of education; they have at their command an appropriate lib-rary, which contains the books necessary to a study of these questions. At the close of the year, each is required to hand in a *mémoire* on a topic prescribed or accepted by the head of the school. On the theoretical side the year is a time of studies distinctly pedagogic. On the practical side, following a time-table drawn up by the headmaster, they attend model or demonstration lessons given by the ordinary members of the school staff. They themselves give criticism lessons . . . which are heard and noted for subsequent criticism by their fellow-students, by the headmaster, and by his colleague who acts as Master of Method. On occasion, they are also employed temporarily as substitutes for members of staff absent from duty, when they also join the Masters' Common Room. In short, they share as much as may be in the life of the school, its recreations, gymnastic exercises and competitions, its school journeys, etc.' (M. Chabot, *La Pédagogie au Lycée*, Paris, 1903).

The details might be vastly different, but one likes to think that Adamson and Chabot would have approved of the spirit behind the Sussex 'tutorial school' pattern. John Townsend shows, in the first section of this book, how the conscious aim behind the experiment *was* to make the first of the tutorial school students really participate in the life of the school. Dick Church was the name of that student. He stayed on as a member of the Thomas Bennett teaching staff, and he has kindly allowed John Townsend to draw fully on the very detailed reports, and exchanges between them, in the first critical year of the scheme.

I arrived in the summer of 1966 when the first 'tutorial school' students were completing their Certificate of Education course. There have been superficial changes, but the essence of the relationship between teacher and student was already there in the first year's dialogue between John Townsend and Dick Church. In the following year, though, we did begin a regular weekly programme of seminars at Sussex University in the spring term: Prussia, however, was never our inspiration. To these seminars would come our dozen students, their half-dozen teacher/tutors, University history colleagues, M.A. research students and colleagues from Brighton College of Education. All the contributors to this book were regular attenders of this seminar. I doubt whether there was an occasion when all were present at the same time, since Culpin came on the course a year after Kendell and Hood. But all three would hear, on different occasions, papers by Frances Lawrence (who was completing her M.A. Degree in Education at Sussex), Peter Mitchell (who was the general supervisory tutor at Thomas Bennett

School of all the students there—non-historians as well as historians) and Colin Brent (who, by 1968, was formally supervising the archive kits which all our postgraduate historians were expected to produce in their year at Sussex).

These seminars—bringing together teachers and students—were more reflective than the down-to-earth seminars of the first term for students only. In the second term we were speculating on the way out of our problems. The structure of the book mirrors this pattern. In the third section, Frances Lawrence, Peter Mitchell and Colin Brent move out from the practical preoccupations of the first two sections in order to examine critically various ways in which the teaching of history may develop in the following years. In the fourth section, I try to assess how far already we have succeeded in taking our young history teachers on, from their experiences of beginning, to a vision of what future—beyond beginnings—is possible in the teaching of our subject.

We would like to thank all the other teacher/tutors and students who shared in our experience, although not in our book. My own debt is profound to Jim Knight who, during the time he was at Thomas Bennett School, along with John Townsend, pioneered this form of training for our historians. Carlos Hood, Chris Culpin and Pat Kendell have not named the schools at which they are now teaching mainly in order not to embarrass their pupils: they have received the most kind co-operation from their respective senior colleagues. We hope that this book will be one with which the prospective young history teacher will be able to identify. Too often he is weighed down with the conviction that he is unique in his failure to handle 3Z or the Corn Laws or both; if this book saps that conviction, it will have done its job.

W. M. L.

NOTE

First names have been used throughout the text. The beginners learned their craft in a school and University that valued informality and spontaneity: it would have been inconceivable for them to have called their tutor 'Mr Townsend', or he to have called them anything but 'Pat', 'Carlos' and 'Chris'. This informality, however, exacted a price. The impact upon the beginner of moving to a more formal atmosphere in a new school was sometimes a rude one.

W. M. L.

I

THE BEGINNERS

John Townsend

POSTGRADUATE students in the school for most of the autumn term: that was unusual. Even more unusual was the knowledge that they would stay for the spring and summer terms as well. This information attracted my attention to the invitation which the University of Sussex sent to the Thomas Bennett School, Crawley, in September 1965 to take part in a new scheme for training postgraduate student teachers. Not only was the training period to be longer than normal, but it was to be school-based rather than university-based, since there was no conventional department of education at the University. Three members of the school staff were asked to operate the scheme. For at least one of them his growing curiosity was accompanied by a little uneasiness at the responsibility he was accepting. The task seemed so nebulous. To get it under way, he would have to work out with his colleagues many practical details; and there were no precedents to help. The University encouraged this activity as the very essence of the scheme. All it would do was to lay down some broad guide-lines.

These provided that for three terms the student would spend two days each week at the University for the theoretical aspects of education, and the other three days at a school where his practical training would be in the hands of a member of staff. This school-based supervisor was required, first, to take his student for a weekly tutorial of one hour; second, to attend each week of the spring term joint seminars of all history students and their supervisors; third, to write a termly report on his student; and fourth, to examine and write a report about one of his essays. Furthermore the University suggested that the student's time in school be divided into three equal parts, one for teaching, another for preparation and the third for note-writing. This last task was given prominence as an important line of communication between student and supervisor. These notes were intended to contain not only brief information about the content and method of a particular lesson, but also the student's reaction to the pupils and his opinion of their reaction to him. In other words he should record his difficulties, his

13

disasters—and his triumphs. What follows, then, is an account of how one supervisor tried to fill in the details of the practical side. The scheme has inevitably a finished look about it, as if it were devised completely at the first attempt. But, of course, it was built up gradually by trial and error, with the help of successive students, some of whom had no hesitation in condemning the more fanciful suggestions put before them!

The Sussex scheme began officially in October 1965, when Pam, Dennis and Dick arrived to start their training, each with an individual supervisor. (In subsequent years a supervisor was normally expected to take two students.) Dick was the student allocated to the History department and thus he embarked unknowingly on an association which was to last well beyond his training year, for such was his progress during that year that he was eventually appointed to the full-time staff. (The same happened to Pam in another department.) He will figure conspicuously in this chapter because he made and filed away copious and critical notes which provide a record of the scheme in operation and illustrations for a number of points raised here. The preliminary information available about him and others was not extensive. The supervisor received, before meeting his students, a report about their performance at the interview for selection for the course, the form completed by them for the Graduate Teacher Training Registry and (usually the most revealing and helpful item) their educational autobiographies written before the beginning of the course. So the first few days in school were concerned very much with the supervisor getting to know his students and deciding what classes would best suit their particular personalities and talents. At the same time the students had the opportunity to look around, to see their allotted classes in the hands of the regular teachers and generally to discover the feel and flavour of the school. Dick's first impressions commended 'the very easy atmosphere', 'the apparently high standard' of the work of a first year form, 'the spontaneous discussion' he found going on in class-rooms. But he was plainly worried about what he felt was the 'terrific noise' around the school, and he very quickly became aware of a fundamental problem facing any teacher: 'how to interest children who just aren't interested'.

What sort of a school did Dick enter? It is a fully comprehensive school drawn from three neighbourhoods in Crawley and thus a student can meet pupils of all ages and abilities. Much attention is paid to the pastoral care of the children through housemasters and tutors. History is taken by all in the first three years and thereafter, until recently, by those who choose it from a number of options for 'O' level or C.S.E. The fourth and fifth years are currently subject to change as a Humanities course, with History as one ingredient, and leading to public examination, is being set up for all pupils. In the sixth form there are two 'A' level courses: the first, English and European, sixteenth and seventeenth centuries; and the second, English Economic History since 1815 and World Affairs since 1939. When the initial allocation of students to schools was first made, their interest and qualifications in contributing to sixth form teaching was a factor that was considered. Apart from public examination forms the student was not tied to a detailed syllabus. For years one to three he was given terminal dates only and was free (subject to the normally easily granted approval of the regular class teacher) to select whatever topics he wished.

The main task of the first term was to see the student settled with classes which were not likely to prevent or retard the building up of his confidence and basic professional skills. If by Christmas he could feel that he was comfortable in front of a class and was doing something purposeful, however elementary, with them, then the aim had been achieved. The bulk of his lessons would be with 'easy' first and second years. The most effective pattern of weekly supervision seemed to be for him to hand in his lesson notes, have them criticised by extensive marginal comments, discuss the notes and criticisms at the tutorial, and be visited in one of his lessons by his supervisor who would then take an early opportunity, perhaps during a morning break, to report his impressions. The visitation was an important check for completeness and for accuracy on the student's own written account of his experiences. It is remarkable how realistic nearly every student was about his performance though the scale and depth of notes have varied very much from one to another.

Dick's files show the difficulties he soon encountered. First, there were what he regarded as personal failings, such as a weakness in remembering names, or too frequent use of 'cumbersome language', or an inability always to answer questions which the class put to him. In short he met with the problems which face every beginner. Soon, too, he had to cope with the particular horror that all students (and many experienced teachers, no doubt) must dread: on 2 November he reported, 'Then the fiasco started. I never visualised running out of material. But so it was.' He seems to have had very few disciplinary troubles. 'Calling out' and 'restlessness' were the worst of his reported trials. But one first-former, Andrew, stood out as a pupil who was not going to be easy to handle. Dick had his ups and downs with him. 'He responded by closing up, resenting me. Odd; he was very well dressed, obviously from a "good" home. Something very wrong somewhere, I think. I must check up.' Two weeks later a sign of success: 'Andrew took a lively interest.' But finally, apparent failure: 'Our friend Andrew forgot his book again.'

It is not possible to recall now how these situations were discussed in the weekly tutorials or what advice was given. The important feature was that Dick was raising his problems and could call for answers upon the experience of an established teacher. To check up on Andrew he would have undoubtedly followed a recommended procedure. This entailed looking first at a collection of notes on problem children, then discussing the boy with his lower-school tutor and finally, if further information was still needed, approaching the boy's housemaster. This investigation would sometimes provide a clue about the right way to handle the child, but often it did no more than enable the student to treat him with sympathy and understanding without discovering how to make him entirely amenable. Sometimes the student might discover a certain member of staff who had a very good relationship with the boy and could use his help. Dick and others were continually reminded that the 'insoluble' problem was a very rare occurrence. Someone in the school or in the University would have the answer and it was the supervisor's task to open up the right channels.

Some supervisory criticisms survive as pencilled, marginal, occasionally inelegant, comments among the notes. Dick, like most students, tended at first to give his classes too much writing to do. 'It still appears you feel every point must have a note. You can safely leave large chunks in a verbal state.' Towards the end of the autumn term he had worked out a routine for his teaching. But then boredom for him and his pupils began to creep in. He was warned: 'Lessons seem to be falling rather into a pattern of explanation, notes, drawing, explanation, etc. Can you vary the method a bit?'; and some suggestions were appended. This advice seems not to have been particularly helpful, for the complaint of 'sameness' was made again a little later. This time the suggested remedy was, 'Could we discuss in detail and in advance your next lesson with III 7?' The uniformity of his technique was not so much a sign of lack of resourcefulness as an indication that he was gaining confidence in himself and had acquired an approach to a group of children which clearly worked. By Christmas he had been accepted by at any rate one class as this report shows: 'Someone said was I coming next term or Mr X, so I said they wouldn't have to put up with me any more; Mr X would be back. This was greeted with groans, "Oh, Sir!" Admittedly my form of words invited them to say this, but I think they meant it.'

Dick's classes were changed each term. This was done partly to give him as wide a range of experience as possible and partly to present him with the incentive of a fresh start. But with later students the change was made at the half-year. The benefit of getting to know better a certain class and being able to follow a longer and more coherent scheme of work outweighed the slight loss of variety of teaching. New classes or not, the student was encouraged from the start of the spring term to make experimentation the theme of his planning. If, like Dick, he was well settled by Christmas, as nearly all the students were, then he was ready to take more 'difficult' classes and to be more adventurous. He needed not so much promptings as ideas. Film-strips, drama, tapes, projects, documents: these were the sorts of new departures that were tried. The bringing together of class, blacked-out room (possibly not the normal teaching room) and projector (borrowed perhaps from another department) formed a good exercise both in organisation and, in the subsequent darkness, in class control best attempted by the student with two or three months' experience behind him.

Above all, the spring term saw the first thoughts about taking a class for an outing. This was an activity for the summer months, but it needed for success a great deal of advance planning. Here, as elsewhere, the student could receive in his tutorials as much preliminary advice as he wanted, but in the last resort the trip was entirely his own affair. Dick's experiences in this area were most instructive. His attempt to take out a first form failed. He must have raised the subject in tutorials, but clearly he did not receive sufficient guidance. His notes tell of the initial enthusiastic response from the class, the ordering of a large coach to cope with this demand, the rapid falling off in numbers when a definite commitment with money was asked for and finally the disappointment of having to cancel the coach. All subsequent students have run very successful outings. But then, unlike Dick, they were well primed in advance with such tips as: expect one-third of the original applicants to drop out; and demand deposits before making a firm booking for a coach.

Dick ran another outing, but this was a short evening one in the school bus and therefore did not need much organisation. The class was a low-stream third form. Nine of them turned up, including Neil (much absence from school, possibly a truant), Alan (on

B

report for bad work and conduct) and Graham (a well-known troublemaker). Soon after the bus moved off orange peel and paper bags were hurled out of the windows. At the destination the boys ran around wildly (like 'taking the dogs out for walks,' commented Dick). Whether the group learned any history that evening is unlikely, but Dick felt that he had learned a lot about them. He was paid two compliments: first, Alan gave him an apple, and second, someone said, 'It was great, sir. When are we going on another one?'

Getting to know the children and seeing them in a situation other than the class-room were two important reasons for the student to organise an outing. Informal talk between staff and pupils is a conspicuous feature of the school and students were encouraged right from the start to join in. Nearly all of them did so naturally and easily, but occasionally a more reserved student had to be reminded to make a conscious effort in this direction, as had one who when asked if he had talked to a remedial Pakistani boy about the football club whose badge he sported in his lapel replied with surprise, 'But I know nothing about football!' To this end of social contact with his pupils, each student was placed with a tutor group which is the basic administrative and pastoral unit in the school. The regular tutor might or might not be in the History department. He was unlikely to be the student's supervisor, for the opportunity was normally taken to give another member of staff some small responsibility for the student's training. Tutors were expected to bring the students usefully into the work of the tutor group, even if, for example, the student was asked to do little more than mark the register on one morning a week. But many tutors discussed the children with the students, talked about those with special difficulties and encouraged student-pupil contacts. Dick was one who sometimes found it difficult to use tutor group time profitably, and at least one of his efforts to make friendly advances to the children met with a rebuff, for 'Kathleen asked me when I was leaving the tutor group. When asked why, she said that I had offended her. She then went on about teachers in general.'

The spring term may have been the time to experiment, but initially it was often a time of setbacks and disappointments. Dick tried out a new idea with one class and reported ruefully, 'Not quite so high a response as I had anticipated.' Then again, 'This was a bad lesson to end an otherwise good day. . . . The trouble is that I don't think the lessons are interesting.' An attempt to start a discussion with a sixth form confronted him with the problem of trying to get the pupils to talk about an unfamiliar subject. In these circumstances the main function of tutorials and lesson-note comments was to show the student where he might make improvements and yet to keep up a high level of encouragement. So after a note complaining about dull lessons with a third form Dick was warned to abandon temporarily the imaginative type of work of which the class had clearly had a surfeit. Encouragement came for him just before the spring half-term when a tutorial comment pointed to '. . . definite signs of real progress now; a little while ago you seemed to have come to a standstill. . . . Your material is much more interesting and directed towards the children's level and interest.'

An important exercise in maintaining the student's confidence and keeping him moving forward was timed for the spring half-term. He was asked to draw up a 'balance sheet' of strengths and weaknesses. These documents were in nearly all cases honestly and perceptively constructed and they provided much material for discussion in tutorials. At the same time the student's educational autobiography was brought up for examination and he was asked to use his own experiences at school as a means of clarifying his ideas about teaching. These discussions were in many cases both interesting and fruitful, not least for the supervisor when called upon to justify his own theories and practices, long believed in and applied unthinkingly.

The student's handling of his classes in the spring term was watched in two ways. First, he was asked from time to time to hand in half a dozen notebooks. These showed the sort of material he was using and enabled the practicalities of marking to be talked over. (Does one correct spelling mistakes? How does one assess: out of ten, out of twenty, by letter grades?) Second, the regular weekly observation of a lesson was maintained. But after half-term, a change was made in the pattern and each class was observed once by its regular teacher who wrote a short report for the supervisor to take up with the student. These reports proved helpful in checking the accuracy of the supervisor's own observations and in throwing new light on the student's performance. In the summer term a fresh idea was for each history student to visit the other's lessons and discuss in a joint tutorial with the supervisor his opinion of what he saw. If the supervisor had laid great stress on encouragement and kindly criticism, this attitude hardly represented the feelings of one student to another! On one occasion only has a student had nothing but praise for a lesson he observed, and this event stands out for its uniqueness. Another rewarding practice in lesson observation was to arrange for an exchange between a history student and a student in an unrelated subject, say biology, with the two supervisors joining in the subsequent reviewing sessions. A number of pertinent comments about materials and techniques usually emerged which observation within the department failed to throw up. This was certainly true for the historians and, one suspects, for the scientists too, for in his knowledge of history the visiting student was often in much the same position as the class, but had the verbal facility to report usefully on the success of the lesson.

The mixing of the history students began in the spring term with the Friday evening seminars at the University, when all the history students, their supervisors and the University subject tutor met to discuss topics both theoretical and practical. The programme for 1969, for example, involved these subjects: history and the primary school, history and the sixth form, marking children's work, integrated studies, the perils of text books, archive kits in history lessons. These occasions encouraged the students to pool their experiences gained in many different types of schools and to receive new stimulus from an outside speaker distinguished in a particular field. In this latter respect two talks from the current (1970) session were memorable. One was from a devoted and highly successful remedial teacher whose exposition was full of practical advice ('Never talk for more than two minutes at a time' and 'You must develop a thick skin'); and the second on the use of documents in history lessons, delivered by an expert whose enthusiasm and obvious teaching skill ('Linger as you unfold slowly the document and rouse them with what an interesting story it reveals about wife-beating') were a model worthy of imitation by any student. Both of these talks provoked interesting discussion which, as on other occasions, was continued in the students' bar after the seminar had been formally closed.

These seminars were not a part of the first year of the scheme. They began in 1966 with the appointment for each subject of a University tutor, known as the 'E' tutor, to bring the University much more into the practical side of the training. News of the impending change caused some dismay among the school supervisors. Was this the beginning after all of a University department of education? Was the whole idea of school-based training, which seemed so full of exciting possibilities and which had roused so much enthusiasm both in the students and in the school, about to be terminated? These fears proved groundless. The University was adamant that the original idea behind the scheme would endure:

the prime responsibility for training remained with the school. In the event a happy partnership developed between 'E' tutor and school supervisor, with frequent exchanges of views and information about the students by letter, telephone and personal contact. Any severe difficulties met by a student could be quickly spotted and taken up. The 'E' tutor made at least one visit in each of the autumn and spring terms to watch the students in action and his observations added yet another helpful assessment of their progress.

In the same year, 1966, the University introduced a second change and this was to appoint a general school supervisor (in the case of Thomas Bennett, the Head of Humanities) who would look after all the students and act as the main channel of communication between school and University. In particular, his function was to hold regular meetings where each student could begin to think about the school and the profession as a whole. This was the opportunity, for example, for the general supervisor to invite the headmaster to discuss, say, school organisation, to answer questions and to meet criticisms. Or what about unstreaming: was this equally feasible in all subjects? Furthermore, some time in the spring term would be suitable for looking at the practicalities of applying for jobs. In short, these general sessions extended the narrower approach of the subject supervisors and provided the occasion for a useful exchange of ideas and viewpoints by representatives of a number of different disciplines. The subject supervisor was always interested to hear from the general supervisor how his own students fared in these meetings. One more valuable area of opinion about them was thus available.

By the end of the spring term, then, the supervisor had built up from a number of different sources a clear and detailed picture of his students. This information was important for their end-of-term progress reports required by the University. The final assessment of the competence of the student depended upon them to a considerable extent. He took no examinations, he was not graded by letter or by class. His fitness to teach was the only fact that mattered and this was decided by a wide variety of criteria. It would not be inaccurate to say that the students really assessed themselves. Of the three reports, that of the spring term seemed the most important. The first, in December, aimed at a quick summing-up of the student and emphasis on those positive features which gave hope for success in the profession. The third, in May, following soon after the spring term report, could usually add little, if anything, to what had previously been written. But by the end of March, of early April, the student's strengths and weaknesses had become abundantly obvious and therefore a detailed and (it is hoped) fair report could be compiled. The University gave at the beginning of the scheme a number of closely defined points for comment, but eventually the supervisor was left free to decide his own framework. Four main headings covered nearly every point that needed mentioning about the history student: character and personality, the classroom, the school, and tutorials. A fifth, general progress, took whatever did not fit elsewhere. The University specified that reports be shown to the student before despatch. This requirement might appear to be inhibiting to the supervisor and possibly embarrassing to the student, but in actual practice, after the initial surprise had worn off, the writer felt quite free to say exactly what he thought and no student condemned as totally unfair anything that he read. If he thought thus he could presumably take up the matter with his University subject tutor.

And so to the last term. At this stage, the supervisor expected that his student had acquired a wide range of materials and techniques, and, through experience of a variety of classes of different ages and abilities, had gained sufficient confidence to handle effectively any group of children. The student himself might not see his position in such a hopeful way. Dick, for example, meeting his first fourth form at the end of April wrote, 'I was nearly shaking before I went in to teach this lot. My entrance was greeted with a variety of interjections generally meaning disapproval.' But he knew no doubt by this time exactly how to react to the situation. Since themes have been suggested for terms one and two, it may be appropriate to call the third term the term of consolidation. The student sensed his growing mastery over the craft and could take pleasure out of exercising and improving his skills. Student Barbara (1969-70), occupied with a sixth form, a fourth form and a second year remedial group, pointed to this condition when she remarked that she was really enjoying the teaching. The supervisor knew that he could do no more for such a student who was then quite fit and ready to take up full-time employment.

Two new tasks arose in the summer term, one for the student and the other for the supervisor. To widen his experience beyond what the school could provide, the student had arranged for him visits to other schools: a primary school, a grammar school run on more traditional lines and a comprehensive school (perhaps a Roman Catholic one, but in any case one clearly different from his training school). By this time the student should have formed some idea of his educational values and should have known what to look for and what questions to ask. The tutorial follow-up to these visits usually centred around two questions: what do they do better than we do here, and why?; and in what ways is this a better school than that one? As in so much of the thinking they were called upon to do in this course, the students showed themselves observant in their appraisals of other schools. Though awkward to fit conveniently into a three-day time-table, these visits proved their worth through the stimulus and quick enlargement of experience they gave the student.

For the supervisor, the summer term provided one more duty to fulfil for the University, and that was to assess and report on one of the student's essays. The subject could be the student's own choice of else could be set by either the supervisor or the University. Barbara (1969-70), for example, wrote on the problems of mixed-ability teaching, and Christine (1968-69) on the place of history in the curriculum with a specimen syllabus added to show how she would translate her opinions into practice. The practical element should predominate in that particular type of essay and any student who drew his ideas entirely from books and failed to use his class-room experience would be penalised. So the report on Christine's essay commended an interesting section where she discussed an investigation she had made into the children's own feelings about history, but faulted her for selecting her practical examples from one class only to the neglect of the wide selection of classes she had taught. Barbara's essay was praised for its handling of the case for unstreaming (her experience showed, for example, that a social mixing did not automatically follow), but was criticised for not even mentioning crucial problems like assessment of work in a mixed-ability group.

One interesting essay was written by Chris (1968-69). This combined theory and practice in just about the right proportions. He had produced early in the spring term an archive kit on Winchelsea. He was provided with a few extra periods, with the scholarship sixth, to try out the kit, and then he decided to take the group to Winchelsea to supplement the maps and documents used in the class-room with some history-on-the-ground. His essay formed the conclusion for this exercise. He began by summarising his aims as a history teacher, went on to discuss the various sorts of source material, including commercially produced kits, and then used the major part of his writing to describe how he put together and tested his kit. A sentence from the report on his essay referred to him as 'a teacher who knows what he is trying to do and has the developing skills to do it'. This could well be the test of a successful essay. It should show that the student had thought about his subject and about his aims in teaching it and that he had some ideas about how to put it across successfully to his pupils.

With the essay assessed and the final termly report written, the supervisor's duties had finished. He might still need in the summer term to help his student to find his first teaching post, but usually he had been appointed during the spring term. The Sussex scheme provided the applicant with two assets. First, he had undergone a long period of training; and second, he had been looked at and weighed up by so many different people, in so many different ways and in so thorough a fashion that it was possible to write a lengthy, detailed and critical reference for him which could deal with every facet of his performance as a teacher. Any appointing body should therefore know exactly the quality of the candidate applying to it.

By this stage, the student was no longer thought of as a 'student', but virtually as a full member of staff. Apart from his shorter attendance each week and his lighter teaching load, he had been asked to do from the very beginning all that was required from a regular teacher. He had taken a tutor group on his own, covered classes for absent colleagues, set questions and marked answers for his classes in end-of-year examinations, written for housemasters short progress reports and the full, formal half-yearly ones, attended departmental meetings, given his opinion about the suitability of third-year children for 'O' level work, or for C.S.E., or for no public examination at all, and accepted a small area of responsibility like keeping a stock cupboard tidy or organising the repair of books. In these circumstances it was not possible to regard the student as someone who was 'different' from or 'inferior' to the qualified members of the department.

By Whitsun, when the course ended, the students had become so much a part of the department that to say goodbye to them had an element of regret about it. The partnership of school, students and University had proved to be both harmonious and stimulating.

2

BEGINNINGS

Pat Kendell

THIRTY-ONE little girls, standing quietly expectant by their desks, eyed me with curious, friendly interest as I walked, brand new register under my arm, to the desk in front of the class. So this was it; here I was with my form L4K.

I can't remember what I said or, indeed, how I got through the first bewildering week of my first teaching post. What I do remember vividly is the chaos of my own thoughts when I reached, thankfully, the end of that first week. I was elated by the friendly reception I had received, but as far as teaching history was concerned I was utterly at sea.

I had spent the previous year discussing the revolution in history teaching which I and my fellow students believed was, or should be, taking place. I now found myself amongst children who accepted the traditional division of their education into subjects and the methods of teaching those subjects. In the school where I did my teaching practice, I had held agonising, but infinitely rewarding, lessons trying to make history exciting and relevant to third-year below-average-ability pupils. (On one occasion one of these children, Sylvia, informed me after spending the whole lesson lolling over her desk still in her outdoor clothes, that she didn't want to learn 'any of that bloody rubbish'.) My new pupils wanted to learn desperately, and in most cases this sprang from genuine interest.

With a sinking feeling I realised that the tables had been turned: now it was my 'exciting' lesson plans which were irrelevant and the problems with which I would have to deal were of a dramatically different kind.

I often wonder what Sylvia and her cronies would have thought of the situation into which I moved. Those anti-intellectual, precocious sophisticates of the modern world, what would they have made of the intelligent minds, cultured voices and the instinctive good manners of my new charges?

What follows is the record of how I have tried to reconcile my ideals with the realities of the situation in which I found myself two years ago. In the process I have changed, or at least modified, many of my ideas, not I hope because I have been crushed by the system, but rather in an attempt to answer the needs of my pupils. One may detect the problems of teaching in a direct grant Grammar School as well as appreciate the advantages.

Outline of the Syllabus and Analysis of Aims as it Appeared Sept. 1968

In general the syllabus up to 'O' level is chronological:

Third form, 11-12 years, Greeks, Romans, Anglo-Saxons, Vikings.

Lower fourth, 12-13 years, British History 1066-1485.

Upper fourth, 13-14 years, British History 1485-1688.

Lower fifth, 14-15 years, British History 1688-Industrial Revolution. (Work from the spring term on includes topics at 'O' level standard in order to ease pressure in the upper fifth.)

Upper fifth, everyone has one period a week in which modern history topics alternate with current affairs.

I have not taught the third form as it is a principle of the school that the Head of Department teaches them in order to get to know them and ascertain their abilities. I shall mention some of the work done in the L4th and L5th, where I work parallel with my Head of Department, but will concentrate on comparing my efforts during the two years with the U4th, as I have both forms and consequently slightly more freedom.

The syllabus outlined above is the familiar history syllabus of most Grammar Schools (note how nicely it fits in with the 'Portrait' series of textbooks published by Oxford.) It can be a meaningless chronological whip-through, but inevitably one has to select topics. In doing so one can simply select topics in which the children are interested, or decide the criteria for such a selection oneself, such as what one wants a class to understand about a particular period.

Whatever the vices of the chronological method of studying history, given the limitation that one must reach a certain point in time by the end of term, how one reaches this point is up to the individual. When I came to this school the traditional syllabus, reign by reign, though still the backbone, had in fact been much mutilated, and apart from the vague aim of giving the children some understanding of British institutions the criteria for this syllabus were noticeable by their absence. However, one thing which was quite clear, was that in the course of their history classes the girls were to be taught various skills necessary for the inevitable academic work of the Senior School (taking good notes, accurate learning, reasoned essay writing) all of which received increased emphasis as they moved up the school.

I think my Head of Department and I are agreed that provided we train these skills, exactly what we teach is up to the individual teacher, although for the sake of convenience the general chronological division is the framework. We are also agreed that the greatest shortcoming in the history taught was that it didn't encourage the girls to think enough for themselves and we concluded that one of our foremost aims would be the attempt to include more primary material to make the children deduce their own conclusions and discourage parrot-fashion learning.

Work with Documents

However academic the children, contact with the raw material of history, be it houses, clothing, pottery or letters, generally rouses their interest and can lead to work in depth. Finding the right material is not easy, but my Head of Department and I were fortunate in coming across a series of letters (see Extract 1 at the end of the chapter) illustrating the way in which a family was divided geographically and ideologically during the American War of Independence, suitable for the L5th age group with whom we study this topic. Letters A and B, we acquired from the Kent Archives Office; it was obvious that Bryan and Phill were related and as we were looking for material to humanise our work on America we were interested. More exciting was the discovery of a postcard reproduction of another 'Martin' letter (letter C); the handwriting and the contents of the letters made it an obvious answer to letter B.

The problem was how to use this material. We made transcripts of the letters and duplicated them, keeping the photostat copies of the originals to hand round for the children to handle and, we hoped, share in the fun of discovering the connection between letters C and B. I can never decide whether it is better to show the originals first and then the transcripts or vice versa, and also how much introduction is needed to the topic. However this is what happened.

The first group with whom I used this material were bright and very keen. They had been used to being given skeletal 'structure' notes on topics, followed by discussion in the course of which I had begun reading extracts from documents and secondary sources. So I began the work on America by a brief résumé of the grievances of the thirteen colonies, which unexpectedly developed into a discussion of colonialism and its problems. I say unexpectedly: in fact, with this group I could never be sure of completing a topic in a given time (an inevitable pressure in a Grammar School when working parallel with another teacher) as they loved airing their views. One child, Jane, though not wishing to take history 'O' level, had a very acute mind and asked questions constantly. She was not always tolerated by the class with a very good grace, but I found her a tremendous asset, as I still do in her U5th current affairs group.

After this I introduced the letters. We spent one lesson simply looking at them, reading them in groups and discussing the technicalities. They were fascinated. One group were especially interested in the deciphering, and helped me with odd words which I hadn't been able to understand. Written work followed. This needed quiet concentration so I gave them questions in class. As you will see the questions vary from those requiring basically factual answers, e.g., 2 and 3, to those requiring careful reading and thought: 1, 6, 7. The letter of reply from Den gave scope for the more imaginative.

The written work was not as good as I had hoped, but their enthusiasm made the development of the scheme worth while. Meanwhile we had discovered another letter (D), which gave more personal details and so with my L5th group last year I was able to emphasise the personalities of the characters more. This worked well as they are a less academic group than last year. Before they answered the more searching questions they drew a family tree and gave little character sketches of the Martin brothers. Their written work was surprisingly good. The people I expected to do well did so, but what pleased me most was the effect upon my problem girl, Linda. As a result of problems at home, this intelligent girl had been in the process of quietly 'dropping out' as far as school work was concerned, she generally day-dreamed through my lessons and trying to get through to her was like trying to reason with the Cheshire cat. However, the Martin family obviously struck a chord somewhere, because her work not only appeared on time, but was substantial and most perceptive. These are some of her answers:

1. I don't think Bryan and Philip Martin are on the same side, and I think this is quite clearly shown in the letters. Bryan has a far more determined and stronger character than Philip, and is quite clearly on the side of the colonists as is shown in a letter from Bryan to his brother Den in England, in which he says 'Virginia is now determined to punish you (Britain) for your crimes'. This is also shown in another letter to his brother in England in which he says that he suspects the English of intercepting his letters before they reach his brother; he says 'I dare not trust to write on matters of great

consiquence.' Philip on the other hand had a far weaker character and though he was officially on the other (English) side from Bryan, I dont think he held strong convictions any way. In a letter from Philip to Robert Fairfax he mentions 'the regiment' and the burning of his military clothes which implies that he was in the British army.

2. The English taylor could get away with selling bad cloth very expensively to the colonists because by law the colonies had to buy English goods and they were not allowed to import foreign goods unless they first came through England.

The colonists felt that this act compelling them to buy British was impractical and extravagant for them, for they could make their own or buy far better quality cloth far cheaper elsewheres. So they decided to try and do without all these things which they were compelled to buy and they were to have only such goods from England as they couldn't live without. Also there was the inevitable smuggling.

3. They regarded the Stamp Act as 'a load under which they were likely to sink' because they thought it would financially ruin them, though I imagine this was gross exaggeration and they were also full of indignation that the British were able to impose these taxes on them.

6. In both of Bryan's letters he suggests that communication was extremely bad between England and America, which it was. It took roughly six months for a letter from the colonies to reach Britain, this is verified when Bryan mentions in a letter to his brother in England dated August, that he has just received his brothers' letter dated in March. In another letter Bryan writes to his mother, 'Phil grumbles at my dress and says I am mad, my coat too long, my hat not fashionable my stockings of an improper colour, nothing right' thus impleing that Bryan who had been in the colonies for about fifteen years was very much behind the fashions of the day again suggesting that communications were very bad.

This fact I think contributed an awful lot to the trouble. The colonists had no direct communication with their Government so they couldn't discuss or argue any point without a six month wait and by that time the situation was sure to have changed.

   8. I think the English were the cause of most of the disputes because they expected the Americans to accept too much discipline. But I think that even if the English had not applied all these laws and acts America would still have found something to rebel about because nearly all the colonists were revolutionary types and had left England as a protest and wanted to break away from England for ever.

She had even shown the work to her mother who was delighted as Linda's apathy had been a great source of worry to her.

In addition to the American letters, we have introduced documents and pictorial material to illustrate conditions in the mills during the revolution in the textile industry. Only a few years ago the L5th *did* the Industrial Revolution: causes; changes in the textile, coal and iron industries; the revolution in transport; results. This year we studied only textiles, bringing in such details of coal and steam as were necessary to understand textile developments. The study has been shaped around documents with the children using text-books for factual details.

The documents used came from a variety of sources: printed collections of documents, archive kits put together by archivists and an excellent one compiled by the Historical Association; plus individual documents from Local Records Offices.[1] The first one which came to hand, the tragic account of the Coulsdon children, is probably familiar to many teachers; but we were delighted when by way of comparison the documents describing the life of apprentice Joseph Sefton and A. Ure's eulogy of machinery appeared. The children could see for themselves that the Industrial Revolution brought relief and improvement in living conditions as well as misery. The study, mainly verbal, developed into a most interesting discussion of the price of progress, and the depth of their understanding and use of documents was apparent in examination answers at the end of term. Whether this will help them with 'O' level answers next year, I rather doubt, as they have little opportunity to reveal the benefit of such studies in depth, but I hope some of them mention the documents when they are answering the old-fashioned 'What were the good and bad results of the Industrial Revolution?'

The result of all this document work (there were others too: Engels's description of Manchester, a list of fines for spinners in the

new mills—which provoked much interest and discussion of the
motives of the mill owners, plus a considerable amount of pictorial
material) was that we did not finish the syllabus this year and,
because of examinations, written work was scanty. We had collected
together several interesting documents to illustrate the Transport
revolution. I was only able to begin using this. Before starting the
topic we looked at a copy of the 1555 Highways Act, and from this
rather amusing document the children were able to deduce for
themselves what were the problems of road repair in the ensuing
200 years. Later I introduced a transcript of a document giving
details of different methods of transport available between London
and Colchester and posed such problems as: 'What do you think
would be the best means of travel for a middle-aged man of
moderate means?' Some most thoughtful answers were produced,
taking into consideration all sorts of factors such as the time of
departure, availability of meals and whether it was better to go
faster and suffer quickly or go more slowly with time for meals
even though the man's digestion might suffer. Most of the questions
were intended to stimulate the imagination and help the child re-
enact the situation and deduce from very few facts a reasoned
answer. Answers to the question: 'Why did the Ipswich Post
Coach cost more and take longer than the Ipswich Machine
Coach?', involved seeing the implications of travelling with the
mail.

You might well say of these lessons described above, 'So what,
haven't we all discussed the use of such material in our training
courses and maybe experimented with it during teaching practice?'
And you would be right. What I managed to do with the L5th
was a drop in the bucket, but in a school of this sort one feels it is
something of a breakthrough because what one comes up against
constantly is tradition and shortage of time. Tradition means that
anything new must work superlatively well in order to be accepted
and one is constantly aware that in a few years these children one
is experimenting with will have to take traditional 'O' and 'A' level
examinations. One can't gamble with their chances of obtaining
good grades in order to satisfy one's own standards of what is good
and interesting in history teaching. Tradition's ally, time, is even
worse; getting through the syllabus is the biggest bugbear of
teaching history in a Grammar School—even in the junior forms.
It is as well to remember that you are most unlikely to get more
than two periods a week (40 minutes each) with each form; these
will probably be separated and in totally unsuitable rooms with no
facilities for model making etc., and if you are a graduate you will

be obliged to give priority to U5th and 6th form work. In my case over half my time-table is devoted to 6th form teaching. This all sounds rather gloomy, but it isn't so bad if one has as sympathetic a Head of Department as I have. Given the limitations of our Grammar School framework, we have done much to enliven L5th and L4th work.

Using documents with the junior forms presents problems. One has to be careful that the difficulty of understanding old English does not create such a barrier as to destroy, rather than create, interest. Furthermore, because of the chronological syllabus one is left with the more difficult Medieval and Tudor material for the younger age groups. Nevertheless I have been able to get over this to some extent.

Domesday Book is of course an obvious example, except that Kent as a county seems to be the exception that proves the general rule. The entry for the Manor of Northfleet was really only useful as an illustration and without preliminary work meant little to 12 and 13 year olds, although this year we used it with some success as a replacement for L4 spring examinations (see below). I have found the *Portrait of the Middle Ages* (in the 'Oxford' series) very useful for the type of child I teach and for much of the Medieval work; I have tried to capitalise on the imaginative powers of this age group.

However, one piece of work, which superficially looks very sophisticated, has gone down quite well and taught the children something very basic about the methodology of the historian. The subject is the mystery surrounding the death of William Rufus. Most children are fascinated by this and love to speculate about how and why it happened. The basis of the work was a sheet of extracts from Medieval and Modern writers giving explanations of the circumstances of Rufus' death. We began by reading the accounts; the children had their own copies and the approach was that of the detective. Each account was discussed and the children made their own notes and sketches. I found one lesson too short to discuss all the possibilities and smaller groups are highly desirable. One group became very intrigued by the fact that according to William of Malmesbury, Rufus' blood dripped all the way to Winchester. They checked with the biology mistress as to whether this was possible if he was in fact dead. This led to a piece of written work entitled 'Who Killed William Rufus?' I explained that they had to refer to the documents for their evidence. Naturally the results were not all closely reasoned and many got carried away by their own theories. This piece by Bridget is typical of the level of reasoning reached by this age group. As you will see she hasn't quoted the evidence but followed her own 'vision' of the event:

Who Killed King William

Well, what is the answer? Did he kill himself or was he killed by someone else? However what we *do* know is that he was shot by an arrow in the New Forest.

We have heard from the various chronicles and historians that various people killed Rufus (as he was called). However I am going to tell you who I think killed him and why?

When William I died he left Rufus, his land in England, Robert his land in Normandy & to Henry he left no land but money.

Rufus & Robert made a treaty together saying that if either of them should die, the other would have his brother's land. It is told that this was done so Henry could not inherit any land of his brothers.

I think that Henry got cross with this & he decided he must somehow get rid of Rufus so that at least he might be quick enough to take the throne from Robert. So this is part of the evidence that was put against Henry.

It says that Rufus was out riding in the forest with Walter Tirel, the King's friend, when an awful looking beast charged towards them & parted the two men from each other.

Then Walter for fear of the beast killing Rufus, shot at it only grazing the animal's back but the arrow rushed on to pierce Rufus sharply in the breast.

Henry saw Rufus's dead body lying on the ground & he ran back to Winchester, demanded the keys from the keeper, to the royal treasury as he said 'I am now the lawful heir'.

More evidence against Henry is that he said he was the lawful heir, but Robert was.

It seems to me that Henry either sent the wild beast running between Rufus & knew Walter would shoot at the beast & he might miss, but this was tricky. The other suggestion was that he bribed Walter to shoot Rufus & to make it seem an accident.

So I think Henry was certainly the culprit.

On the other hand Philippa, a more intellectual and better disciplined child, produced this well reasoned piece of work, if rather one-sided:

How was William Killed

I think that the most likely explanation is the one put forward by Ordericus Vitalis, who says that Henry and several companions went with William and Tyrel, and implies that the master mind of the plot (if it was a plot) was Henry, William's brother. Vitalis says that as soon as Henry saw the dead body of his brother he went straight away to Winchester, and demanded the keys of the treasury, as rightful heir to the throne. Vitalis also says that it was Tirel who shot the arrow which killed the King, and it is known as a historical fact, that when Henry became King he bestowed a lot of money and land upon Tirel and his family. All this points to the fact that it was Henry behind it all, and that he asked Tirel to kill the King in return for land and money. I also think this is the most likely explanation because Henry had quite a few good reasons for wanting his brother dead.

The first, and perhaps most obvious, reason is simply because he wanted the throne and the kingdom.

The second, is because he hated his brother. (Perhaps he comforted his concience with the thought that he was doing it for the good of the people!)

And the third is because his brothers William and Robert had excluded him from the treaty about their land.

I have thought about the evidence and I think this is the most feasible theory.

I do not regard this experiment as a great success. Next year I will try dividing the class into groups; give each group a different account, and ask them to tell the story either with the aid of drawings or as a dramatic sketch for the rest of the class to see. This could be followed by a class discussion and written work. However, the material itself teaches two important lessons especially relevant to the academic child: *a*, that people who write history do not always know the true facts, and *b*, if they do, they can slant the truth.

Although the use of documents is limited with this age group, maps and castle plans hold great possibilities and require less preparation. Mary Price's *Middle Ages*, has a good aerial photograph of Conway among the plates at the back of the book. This together with plans of Conway Castle in *The Medieval Castle* ('Then and There' series) and the material supplied with the B.B.C. programme on Edward I and Wales (an excellent series called 'Decisive Events in British History') have provided the basis of studies on town life, castle life and how and why Edward I conquered Wales.

I have not used much unpublished archive material with the U4ths, i.e. Tudor and Stuart material, because a lot of really first rate accounts have already been published. For example the edition of *They Saw It Happen* covering this period is a treasure-house. I used it constantly, but will mention only one document here: the account of the taking of Edward Campion. The children knew something of Elizabeth's religious settlement and why Roman Catholics were disliked. I began the lesson on Campion by drawing on the board a plan of the room where he was hidden before his capture and death. The children knew about priest holes, many of them had seen them in country houses during holiday visits, and they were fascinated by the practical details: how was the room ventilated? how long could they survive? and what did they eat, etc., etc. Most of all they wanted to know why Campion didn't escape via the stairs under the moat. Lots of suggestions were made and as it was the end of the lesson they were left speculating! Next lesson I handed round the account by Elliot and they soon dis-covered that the moat had been surrounded by the J.P.'s men. This extract is good because it leaves lots of room for speculation and several children pointed out that the half-hour the men were kept waiting outside the gates was highly suspicious, and they thought Mrs Yate ought to have thought of some better excuse. The written work resulting from this indicates, I think, the degree of imaginative involvement possible in this type of work. This is an extract from one child's work; she is most intelligent and imagina-tive and really lives her history as you can see:

> I ran to the window & glanced out. Sure enough, there towards the castle galloped armed men & in front was Elliot. I recognised him because of his black moustache & purple doublet. I froze with horror & the room swam before me. What could I do? I must hide the priests, for these men had surely come to find them. 'Quick!', said I to Mary; the housemaid 'Run down to the gate house & tell the porter to keep them out until I come. Run, girl!' No sooner had I said this, than she was out of the room, running to the gate. I ran into my dressing room & rummaged through the chests until I had found three dresses & head wear. Throwing them over my arm, I hurried downstairs & went into the room which housed the nuns. I found them praying. I waited reverantly, a few minutes, then interrupted them & beseeched them to

change from there nun's attire into the dresses I had brought.
I left them to change. As I hurried to the priests, I met Jane,
a friend of mine who was staying in the house. She told me
that, the men had surrounded the moat. I was dumfounded.
What could I do now? I had hoped to smuggle the priests &
nuns out, in the passage which led under the moat. Now, I
was not able to. These government agents were clever. I
asked Jane, to go to the kitchens & fetch enough bread, meat
and drink for three or four days & bring it upstairs. Then, I
went to the priests & asked Edmund Campion, who was one of
them, to follow me upstairs, quickly. All this time I could hear
banging on the gates. I could not keep them out much longer.

*   *   *

Everything was hidden now & I straightened my dress &
tried to stop panting. Accompanied by Jane, the disguised
nuns & five gentlemen who were staying with us, I walked
sedately to the gate, bidding the porter open it.

'Good morning, my dear Gentlemen. What brings you
here in such a hurry? I must apologise for keeping you waiting
so long. But, as today is Sunday, my household is very slack.
I must admit, my friends & I have hardly been up for long.
The maids are very lazy & do not bother to answer, they
leave it to the porter, who unfortunately is deaf. Pray, do
come in. May I offer you some victuals?

They searched the house while I sat in a chair and pre-
tended to continue my tapestry. Every minute I expected to
hear a cry and running feet, going towards that hollow wall
upstairs. I must seem completely at ease. One nervous glance
at the wall, one furtive whisper to Jane, might give them
away. I sat in this state of nervousness all day. Until, at dusk,
they left. At last, I could relax. But still I did not dare look
in the secret rooms. One man might have stayed to spy. I
glanced out of the window, my heart sank, I could see
twinkling lines around the moat. They had not given up. I
could not smuggle the priests out, still. All night was spent
in nervous wakefullness.

The only unpublished document I have used was an account of
the death of the Duke of Buckingham by Edward Dering, a
Kentish gentleman whom one of our sixth form was studying for
her 'A' level project. She brought the document to me, and having
transcribed the rather poor photostat, I was able to read it with the

U4th. They were intrigued by the story of its origin, but apart from the dramatic 'Villain, thou hast stabbed me!', the language was too difficult for them and even the most intelligent found such sentences as, 'My shallow capacity or else my slender intelligence could never deceive unto my undertaking a knowledge, or unto my mind a belief of the 100th part of his plots against this state . . .' difficult to deal with. However, several, as with the L5th, found the manuscript problems interesting and one child took home the photostat to work on a couple of words I couldn't decipher.

Because the drama and immediacy of the Campion account are not always present in contemporary documents, I have made much use of secondary accounts because I am sure that inspiring interest is more important at this age than maintaining academic accuracy.

For example Hester Chapman's account of the last hours of Jane Grey's life is most moving and reads dramatically, holding one U4th form spell-bound for fifteen minutes. In a slightly different vein there is a delightful account of the Field of the Cloth of Gold in Scarisbrick's *Henry VIII*. This piece, rich in information about Henry and Wolsey, was a very useful introduction to study of these two men. It also lends itself very well to visual work. Some children produced maps of the site as Wolsey might have drawn it whilst others did delightful pictorial stories.

In my attempts to introduce as much primary material as possible, I have relied mainly on documents because lesson time and poor display space makes the use of other artifacts more difficult. Moreover because these children are essentially verbally and academically orientated, it seemed sensible to begin with written material which would tap their ability fully and also stimulate their imaginations. However, one experiment using visual material which has some success was the use of wall pictures to illustrate the development of painting during the Renaissance period. I had found dealing with this topic very difficult in my first year because I couldn't strike the right level; either I was far too obscure or ludicrously over-simple. The next year I decided to tackle the subject through painting and then a study of Leonardo da Vinci, and leave it at that. This method was more successful because whereas at the end of the first year several children specifically mentioned the Renaissance as a subject they had not enjoyed, in my second U4th group eight people said they had enjoyed it, especially Leonardo da Vinci. I suppose this is an improvement on nil.

To begin this series of lessons I arranged wall displays of contrasting pictures. For example on one sheet I had paintings of the 'Madonna and Child' by Cimabue (still essentially Medieval);

Van Eyck (Northern European, showing some Renaissance influence); and Michelangelo (Italian, High Renaissance). There were three such sets of pictures and each had questions underneath, e.g., How do the backgrounds differ? Which baby do you think is the most babylike? How is the use of colour different? The children moved round in groups and then we discussed their observations and they probably learned as much from this as a formal lesson on the changes which the Renaissance brought. This was much helped by the fact that concurrently some of them were having history of art lessons with the art mistress. I was delighted by this link-up and would like to pursue the possibilities, but again one comes up against barriers of time and syllabus structure.

Examinations are another problem which we have endeavoured to modify lower down the school by the use of documents. This is not the place to discuss the examination system in our secondary schools, but helpless though we felt in face of 'O' and 'A' level pressures, we did feel we could introduce internal examinations which emphasised understanding as well as accurate learning. Thus this year's L4th did not have a spring examination but instead during one lesson they studied the Domesday entry for Northfleet Manor, answering questions involving an intelligent understanding of the document itself as well as a general knowledge of the topic studied during term time. I did the same thing with the U4th; in the spring term they had two documents, one describing Henry VII and the other the Dissolution of Glastonbury Abbey and in the summer term one document and an essay in order to prepare them for the L5th pre-'O' level examinations. The results were interesting, and unlike the previous U4th groups I taught, no one said they 'hated the exam', indeed most seemed to have enjoyed it. Along with the Tudor educationalist Roger Ascham I believe that what is enjoyed is most likely to be retained.

I am very aware of my lack of adventure in the use of slides, filmstrips and tape recordings. But the use of such technical aids is restricted by the 40-minute periods, old-fashioned plugs and a shortage of good 'soft ware'. Our money allowance is eaten up by the purchase of books (and examination work is of course given priority). What filmstrips we do have are very poor quality and I find showing such films simply produces amusement amongst children used to TV and cinema standards, however good the actual material. For example a film illustrating the Renaissance which I showed in connection with the pictures described above was tolerated, but not enjoyed because of the poor reproduction. However, we are beginning to tap the possibilities of tape recordings.

My Head of Department has taped several of the B.B.C. 'Decisive Events' programmes as we cannot fit in with the times of broadcasting, and one in particular went down very well. This was a dramatisation of the War of American Independence, which I used after the Martin letters study. It was an excellent way of dealing with the war, which can so easily become a tedious list of battles. Whilst listening, I asked them to think about the way the American colonists eventually won the war and to make their own notes. This, together with their own reading (I gave them guidance as to headings) enabled them to write competent answers to an 'O' level question on the war, without tedious dictated notes from me. If one had more time during the U5th year to develop this method for a more highly selected 'O' level course, this examination might actually become fun to teach and take.

Using tape recordings, records etc., has opened up great possibilities, but they must be absolutely suitable and edited if necessary. I feel the lack of technical knowledge here and inevitable lack of time to experiment. But nothing is worse than playing something which bores children: it's even worse than an overdose of one's own voice.

One final point; in a school of this sort one doesn't feel the necessity to educate the children culturally as with more socially deprived children, and consequently very few school visits to places of interest are arranged; it is the children themselves who bring to school information, in all shapes and forms, of their family visits and experiences; this is interesting and occasionally very useful. For example, when we were studying the photograph of Conway, deciding where the entrance gates were was not easy. Fortunately, Catherine (sister of Anne, mentioned later) had visited the town and was able to help us. However, I would like to make visits and base lessons around a family house, e.g., the Verney home at Claydon. I am very envious of the school which was able to take over an old cottage and re-enact the way that people lived in the eighteenth century,[2] but the disruption this would cause simply makes impossible such a project: one missed lesson with the U6th could be vital. Such are the realities. Moreover, the time and research needed in preparing this exercise can end in disappointment. I was very keen to get hold of some of the Verney manuscripts, and wrote to Claydon only to learn that all the Verney documents are now on microfilm, only to be seen at the British Museum or in Buckinghamshire Records Office, which of course doesn't open on Saturdays. Undaunted, I decided to visit the home: delightful though this was I was depressed to find virtually no signs of the original house, and so my great ideas were reduced to using *Cavaliers and Roundheads* ('Then and There' series) which bases the story of the Civil War around the Verneys.

As the introduction of source material has played a large part in my teaching endeavours, I was heartened to read Gareth Jones' description of one of the principles of studying history as 'getting down to the grass roots by studying the raw material of history, documents as well as other types of sources and attempting to interpret them'. But he also said, 'Historians study history because they want to find out what happened in the past'.[3] This is so true of the school child-historian and in the following section are some details of the ways in which I have tried to capitalise on children's curiosity and involvement in the re-creation and re-living of historical events. This is just as important for Grammar School children as less able children.

Imaginative Work

Much of the imaginative work the children do for me results from the study of first-hand accounts such as that on Campion described above. But there is a place for imaginative re-creation of events using less detailed and accurate accounts, if only because it involves children, especially the less academic who haven't always a natural interest. (We do have such children amongst the fee-payers; many of whom would not be in a Grammar School as a result of 11 plus selection.)

Perhaps the most interesting example of this is the work of the U4th on life in an Elizabethan village. The only material available on this was the chapter in their text-book, which though containing a lot of interesting information was not very exciting. To make it more interesting I duplicated a plan of a medieval village, such as they were familiar with from the L4th work. Each child had a copy and they were asked to find out all the ways in which the village had changed (using their text-book and common sense) and then to draw the same village 300 years later, explaining their changes with the help of a key. They could make any changes they liked provided they gave a sensible reason; the names of the villagers, etc., were entirely left to them. I gave very little introduction to this work, apart from explaining briefly what an enclosure was; instead I answered questions as they arose.

Some of the resulting work was very good, but it was on the whole the more academic and interested who had produced the better work although it had given scope for the artistic too. I wanted something more than this and so with the one form, marginally less academic and more bouncy than the other, I tried something quite different. We had by now established that the worst kind of enclosure was that of the common land (I had read Thomas More's piece about the sheep eating up the people, which they found very funny) and so we set about dramatising such a situation in the village of Woodham. Parts were given out and I gave them ten minutes or so in which to work out the arguments they would bring forward at a meeting in the village when the lord's decision to enclose was challenged. There was much giggling as they decided their names and who was whose wife etc., whilst the lord practised strutting around. To bring some order (I hoped) into a potentially chaotic situation, I appointed Anne, who was rather good at bringing order amongst her classmates, as leader of the village delegation. Quite honestly I was amazed how well it went; Anne stamped and shouted to keep order as cries about 'our children', 'my poor cattle', issued from the crowd. Philippa as the priest was excellent and brought some rationality into the emotional pleas of the others. The lord, his sons and followers, had a really hard time of it, and the whole thing became so heated that at one point Alison (the lord) having failed to convince the priest of the economic necessity of enclosing the common land, hissed at me, in desperation, 'What shall I say now?' What with the noise and the heated nature of the discussion, we failed to hear the bell and it was not until the L4th, with rounded eyes, pressed at the door, that we had to finish. This discussion continued down the corridor.

This was one of those rare moments in teaching when one feels that it is really worth the effort after all. The historical accuracy of this drama is to be doubted, but I felt that these children would always remember that enclosures involved people and people's feelings and was not simply a 'movement' in the inevitable process of economic development. It was a very spontaneous occasion, they had relatively no time to prepare it, and the group on the whole was temperamentally suited to such an experiment. But this is part of the mystique of teaching: discovering the right methods for different groups.

I have attempted few other dramatisations, because quite simply the right occasion has not arisen. But the children themselves have written dialogue, quite often spontaneously as part of written work. The most moving was that by Philippa about Joan of Arc (written the year before her performance as the priest). This is the last scene from this play in two acts, when having been condemned as a heretic by the French, Joan is handed over to the English.

Prosecutor: Joan, you are brought here on a charge of witchcraft, firstly because you fortell the future, which as everyone knows comes from the devil, secondly because you have employed the help of the feind to pursue your evil purposes.

Have you anything to say?

Joan: What is the point of speaking? This is only a mock trial. Whatever I say will make no difference. But, may I ask is not fortelling the future the same as phrophesying, and did not the phrophets of the old testament prophesy? I know what your answer will be already—that is a different matter. But is it a different matter? Were not they persecuted? Did they not have to suffer for their beliefs?

Pro.: My lord, her own words damm her. She is comparing herself to the prophets. This surely proves not only heresy, but witchcraft for she is trying to get around us, pretending she is a Christian. Do not heed her words my lord.

Joan (wearily): If I were a witch would I not employ all my powers of witchcraft to spirit me away. But what is the use of arguing? You are all firmly convinced in your mind, were firmly convinced before you came that I am a witch.

Judge: Have you anything to say, defender?

Defender: Nothing, my lord. It seems that I was wrong in wanting her to defend her.

Joan: 'The cock crew, and Peter realizing what he had done, wept out loud.'

Def. (Nervously): What did she say that for.

Judge: This court has found the defendant to be guilty of witchcraft. Therefore I sentence you to be burned by a fire until you are dead.

Joan: Sweet Jesu, give me courage. I am afraid desperately afraid. Oh God, God, don't let them kill me! Lord, lord, why hast thou forsaken me. (She falls to her knees) Lord I can't die, I'm too weak. I can't bear pain.

(There is a long silence, then she slowly rises, no longer white and pale, but triumphant).

The lord has given me courage. I will die as bravely as I can, for the pain will seem but little compared to the bliss of seeing our lord, our God, face to face. My lord, I thank you. You are not condemming me to death but to eternal life.

(There is another long pause. Then everyone stands as the Judge walks out in silence. Everyone follows as before.)

We had a reading of it in class, but it obviously lacked the spontaneity of the village drama.

Writing poetry is a form of dramatisation which L4th and U4th age groups enjoy and do much better than older children because they are less self-conscious and less self-critical. I have noticed that those children who are more limited and less able to write at length, produce the best results. The first poem, on King William I, is by a child who generally gets B to B— grades for written work, whereas the second is by a very talented child, Rachel, who is passionately interested in history and writes, for fun, sketches and plays on historical topics with her equally talented friend Jessamy. That on the Armada is by an older, abler child; I think she has reproduced the ballad form rather well.

William I

When William the first
Set foot on the coast
He swore and cursed
And frightened his host.

He frightened his host,
For being in haste
He got a nose-bleed
For he triped over his lace.

He won a great battle
And ruled over Britain.
He claimed all the cattle
An' stoped us just sit'n.

We worked for his people
And fought in his battles,
We builded his steeples
And gave gifts to his people.

He wrote a big book,
Domesday by name.
In which he could look
To see what he gained, apart from his faim.

When Harold of England the North-men did fight;
To Pevensey came William, a harsh cruel knight.
He proclaimed that Earl Harold in Normandy swore
To give him our island when the king was no more.

Ah foreign tongued William, you care not for us
It is just for the crown that you make such a fuss.

As Harold drew nearer, you took up your stand
At Battle, and fought for the right to our land.
With slyness you drew us into a marsh
And then cut us all down in a manner most harsh.

Ah foreign tongued William, you care not for us
It is just for the crown that you make such a fuss.

Then a fateful stray arrow struck the king in the eye
He fell and was axed and thus did he die.
Now William's our master, and taken our land
To give to the Normans and noblemen grand.

Ah foreign tongued William you cared not for us
It is just for the crown that you made such a fuss.

Be Warned!

The scene was set upon the sea
In fifteen eighty eight
The 'Dons' were sailing in their ships
To conquer us. They came.

They had an hundred ships and more
And sailed right up to France.
Said Drake, 'Send fireships after them.
We'll make those Spaniards fly.'

We took some oil and tar and ships,
(The two we poured within).
And in the night, we set them light
And sailed the fireships in.

They wrought great havoc in the fleet
They burnt up all they touched.
The sky was red, the sea was hot
Great timber floated there.

Two choices lay before the foe—
To sail away, or be
Destroyed by us—the British Fleet.
The best men on the earth.

They sailed away—away from France
Then hopes of conquest gone.
We chased them round to Newcastle
Then stopped right there to land.

The Spaniards sailed away off North,
To risk the rocks and sea.
They could not stand up to the strain
Of brave, bold Englishmen.

The scope for story writing is of course limitless and we are all familiar now with the 'Imagine you're a . . .' approach. I have had some really excellent work because the children have ability and are encouraged to write in this way in their English lesson. There is a danger with children of this sort, in that being disciplined and intelligent they are able to write what is required, technically faultless, but fail because there is a lack of feeling. This doesn't very often happen but when it does I feel very depressed. The pieces included do, however, show feeling. The first is written by a highly imaginative girl and, although rather sentimental for sophisticated minds, does have genuine feeling, and this by a child who started out being most unco-operative and querulous.

Memories of Edward VI
(By Barnaby Fitzpatrick)

A year has gone by now: a year since Edward's death. Since I have been at court, I have spent such a lonely time, but soon the permanent grief I have been living under will wear off. It must; for I cannot live as a person always dreaming of yesterday, Never tomorrow.

Sometimes, I sit, head in hands, dreaming of old times. My eyes see a quiet river, and then the face of a serious, pious boy, who is speaking gently, and gesticulating. He is telling me of his tiring day and how he wishes some days he could relax. But he knows in his heart he never could relax, for his mind is always working, working. When we have our lessons, I am content to know that such a word in Latin means something, in English, but Edward must know

English derivations, and other Latin words connected to the word. Indeed his want of curiosity often dumbfounded Sir John Cheke, his favourite tutor, especially in matters of geography his pet subject. He outclassed me at this so much; I hardly doubted he was a genius; but I know now it was his unsatiable desire to know about the world he lived in.

Now, I see his mouth moving gently and his grey eyes looking tired and dull. He runs a hand through his thatch of fair hair and sits down on a tree trunk, mossed and covered with lichen. He starts to talk of his days doings, and what ambassador he will have to entertain that evening.

He tells me how he got up late that morning, despite the bright sunlight and was so late for mass. However; he says it did not matter for the sermon had not started. Now his face is alive and eager as he tells me of the sermon about Luther. Then we are both talking of lessons. I am saying with mock seriousness that it is beneath a king's dignity to scatter blotting sand on the floor. Strangely, I see his face glow shamful, then lighten as he realises I am joking. There is a hush, and then we break it by talking of other lessons, Latin, greek, geography, french, german and divinity. Once again; the Lutheran religion and the new prayer book Edward is interested in.

Then he tells me of the state affairs and how they (he and the Privy Council) have a problem. But he changes the subject for he never imparts state troubles home. Slowly, we shift off to the steps leading down to the river, and Edward talks of ships, spices and life at sea. He is explaining about rigging to me when the mists begin to come down, and as we laugh heartily at a slip of the tongue, he begins to cough. It is a deep and throaty cough and in my dreams I see my anxious, puckered face. He has another coughing fit, and I say there is a chill in the air.

My eyes take on a gloomy look as I see him, playing his lute, his mind no longer with us, but far, far away.

I tear myself away for I know what the next scene will be; I cannot stop it coming before me—the young king on his death bed at the age of sixteen.

Obviously this caught her imagination. The second piece, written by a less able child from the literary point of view, is in many ways better. The style is more original and she has managed to convey Edward's character rather well.

A Possible Extract from a diary by Edward VI

Sunday 14th November. 1548

I attended a three hour service at Westminster today. Very interesting especially the sermon. 5 psalms, 4 hymns and 3 complete anthems, the choir is very good. I have heard that the Spanish Ambassador is planning to visit us, this is a little awkward as he and the French Ambassador, who is with us now, do not always agree. Barnaby and I walked in the palace gardens for half an hour this evening. My cough is a little better but is still troublesome. Master Cheke says we can study astronomy tomorrow, geography as well if there is time.

Monday 15th November.

It is true that the Spanish Ambassador is coming and sooner than we expected, but unfortunately the French ambasador has decided to leave in a few days. I am very tired and I have hardly seen Barnaby today. My physician says he cannot do any more to stop my cough becoming worse. I enjoyed an hour studying astronomy this morning.

Tuesday 16th November.

Master Cheke has a slight cold and cannot teach me today. There are two piles of papers from the Privy Council that I shall have to read and sign, this is interesting but I get so tired. There will be a farewell feast and ceremony for the French Ambassador tomorrow.

Wednesday 17th November.

Master Cheke's cold is better. I do not understand one of the papers I received from the privy council. So I think I shall ask Master Thomas to explain, I shall have to send the note with great care, for if my uncle, Somerset, were to see or hear of it he would be very angry. Master Cheke says my Latin could be better but he praises my Greek and French.

Thursday 18th November.

The feast yesterday went on until one in the morning and I had to be dressed by eight to see the French Ambasador off. It was a great relief to see him go as the Spanish gentleman arrives this afternoon. Sir Nicholas has brought a note from Master Thomas explaining what I asked. Barnaby is very worried about my cough, which is worse, but I wish he would not fuss so.

Friday 19th November.

I did not go to bed last night, the Spanish ambassador has arrived with his retinue. My Gentlemen of the Bedchamber are arguing about the tapestries in my room. Barnaby and his followers want red but the rest are sure blue would be best. Barnaby has his birthday today, but I did not know what to get him because he has all he asks for anyway. I am very tired and my cough is worse. State matters are pileing up but I must look after the ambassador before I attend to them.

Project Work

Ideally I would like to do far more projects with children working either in groups or on their own, but the scope is limited at the moment. However teaching both U4th forms has given me more chance to select topics from the syllabus and arrange the work more freely.

I find that I have to be careful teaching parallel forms the same work and have endeavoured to avoid teaching the same topic in the same week, or tried to vary the method of presenting the material. For example, whilst one form worked on a board display of Henry VIII, his wives and descendants, each child having a particular character to find out about, I taught the other group more formally with a lot of readings and anecdotes about Henry's wives which are always enormously popular. Interestingly the group who did the board display, good though it was, never really thought they had learned much about the characters other than the one they did, and so although their work was more active, and many teachers would say better educationally, the other group derived more satisfaction in the end.

Teachers converted to the enquiry-based methods might well criticise the fact that I 'tell' the children too much. I do so if the topic lends itself to this more dramatic approach, or if I feel their enthusiasm will be dampened by being told to work on their own. The atmosphere of wanting to learn is so important and so easily destroyed. Generally I don't feel the need to stimulate enquiry, it comes readily. What I feel is more important in my school is guiding the children to select and use the facts which they hunt up or ask for. Consequently I am dubious as to the value of the type of project where the child sets out to find all he or she can about a particular person or event. Unless one is very careful one simply ends up with a lot of neatly, or not so neatly, copied out information which obviously means very little to the child. The Jackdaws, great break-through though they are, often worsen this situation. Too many of them do the work for the child, not only in providing the information, but in giving ideas as to presentation and layout, which tends to over-influence even the most original child. Kits of this sort would be better if, as with many now being produced by local records offices and especially those produced by the Historical Association, they simply provided the raw material with transcripts and, where necessary, some indication as to importance, use, value, etc. This might be best done in question form and possibly by the teacher because only she can judge the capability and needs of the child concerned. We found this with the kit on Essex Roads referred to earlier. (I should emphasise how much I welcome all these kits; my criticism applies only to them being used by the child as a new type of text-book, which they are not. Perhaps the main barrier to their proper use is that there are insufficient copies of the documents included to hand round and use as the basis of lessons.)

I have tried overcoming the problem of copying by giving the class broad questions, e.g. 'Think what the man or event you are studying tells you about the eighteenth century', or whatever; by limiting the number of words to ensure they have time to think about the topic; and most important by trying to see each child and ensure she is asking the right questions. Suggestions such as, 'Invent a family around which to describe medieval life or changes in fashion 1700-1800', can bring to life what might otherwise be a meaningless catalogue. One child, who did the latter, produced a most interesting project tracing developments in fashion through four generations of an imaginary family.

However, far and away the most interesting project work were the newspapers done by the U4th. This is of course by no means an original idea, but in my particular teaching situation it worked very well. One form wrote theirs to celebrate the accession or coronation of Elizabeth and the other form recorded the death of Mary Stuart. This helped to ease demand on the books, and overcame my problem, mentioned earlier, in teaching both forms. Before they began I gave them some suggestions as to layout; questions to guide them in their reading and, I hoped, dissuade them from copying out of books; and a book list, handing out bits and pieces that I had collected together.

This type of project is good because it gives the children a definite structure and at the same time leaves the gate wide open for them to pursue their own interests. For example, the musical children produced all sorts of interesting details about Byrd and Tallis with advertisements for contemporary musical instruments.

D

Others found out about literary figures, and were amazed to discover how late Shakespeare began writing. I had articles about Italian artists and intellectuals, warnings about the Spaniards, biographical notes on Elizabeth's advisers, cookery recipes and medicinal remedies. The children produced books, guide-books, postcards, and the help they received at home made me realise how much easier it is teaching children whose parents are so cooperative.

In a very simple way these girls were doing their own research, seeing links between subjects for themselves and above all, asking questions. I found the lessons quite exhausting, trying to answer questions, and even more difficult, asking *them* questions. I think these were some of the pleasantest hours I've spent in school: being involved, together, in finding out and creating.

Another point about this particular project is that it allowed each child to find her own level, and several less able children produced newspapers which were both good to look at and interesting to read. Anne (of the play), whose academic work is generally very poor, was able to make the most of her somewhat racy, undisciplined style producing a paper, which though not very accurate in detail, posed searching questions in true journalistic fashion. I do not wish to imply that this is good historical writing, nor indeed, that Anne will ever be an academic historian. But she enjoys her history and has, I hope, grasped that history is more than facts set out in a text-book. (See extract 2 at the end of the chapter.)

*   *   *

I have now completed two years of my apprenticeship in the teaching profession. Two years ago I was passionately concerned about teaching methods—*which* were good and *which* weren't—especially in relation to history teaching. I still care, but I am less worried about the method and more concerned about the result. I haven't been able to put into practice many of the ideas I had in 1968 and would love to have time to prepare lessons involving other subjects. I would like to move right away from the formal classroom image with the desks in rows and blackboard in front, organising instead expeditions, work in libraries, museums, records offices and interviews with people in the local district. There have been moments of great depression as well as moments of elation, possibly the experience of most teachers all their careers. It is intensely frustrating when a beautifully conceived lesson flops and unthinking children make wounding remarks. It is most exhausting stimulating children to think for themselves; teaching children *what* to think is so much easier. Then there are all the restrictions: traditions, examinations, and lack of time.

But the rewards are many: the child who suddenly begins to show interest like Linda; the child who lingers after a lesson to ask questions; the hush in a room when all present are completely absorbed; the new ideas of fresh minds: the fun of learning together.

EXTRACT I

A

Letter from Philip Martin to Robert Fairfax on the bitter antagonism to the Stamp Act 1766. (*Reproduced by permission of Kent County Council from the Kent Archives Office.*)

Greenway Court Aprill 30 1766

Dear Sir

I cant help repeting what you have so often heard the confusion this Country is in on account of the stamp Act they are impatient to know there destiny whether they are to sink under a load they say is imposible for them to surport or once more to be a happy People our anxiety is great as it is a thing of no small concisquence hear. I have received all that could call to my share they have birnt all my military Cloaths at New York I left them as I was told I should run a risk of loosing them as they went through the Country, but that is trifling to what it will be hear if the Law is not repealed.

My Lord is very well and gone on a visit for a fiew days to Belsay as it was left to our choyse. Tom and I declind going for reasons you shall know when I have the pleasure of seing you. I have not heard anything from the Regt since my arrivall to prevent Conl Belford having an opertunity of saying I did not apply to him I rote sum time ago to have my leave renewd, but hope you will not forget me as you was so kind to say you would have sum thind don before my leave expird and wish the exchang could be to cum to England. Tom rote to you last month and desired his duty I am

Dear Sir your Affectionat
Nephew
P Martin

B

Letter from Bryan Martin to his brother the Rev. Denny Martin referring to anti-English feeling in America. Aug. 1769.

Your letters dated in March came to hand, which is all I have received neither have I heard from Phil this Summer, you tell me you are certain that our letters are not intercepted on your side the Water dont be too confident as I differ with you in opinion, I wish I could be with you a few hours, I dare not trust to write on Matters of great consiquence, let me add that we have a Friend Resolute, Steady and immoveable, neither to be changed by Art, or threats, Patience he has and more than a common Stock is necessary, I am a Stranger to ease and content both are banished from hence, Politics daily gives rise to our disputes tho not the real cause, as we end with private Affairs with great Severity— The B— a Warm Advocate for American liberty and an Enimy to English in positions generally concludes by adding You damnd English are become baggers by your Extravagance and want to make Us the same————— My Lord desires you will send him a neat plane Harness with Chains for Six Horses, to go Single the Collers for Horses fourteen hands and a half high, Spare Thongs, & Buckles, to be made by Muddle of Harrison, apply to A——es for the Money, forget not that you are executing the Commands of a Sincere Friend——

Inform Depiene your Taylor that he uses me ill by vending bad Cloths at a most Extravigant Price, I suppose he concludes that any thing is good Enought for us Virginians he has lost my Lords Custom by imposing on me.

My Lord and Mr Fx— are going to spend some weeks at Our Bath. Mr Fx looks Well and the Climate Agrees with him, he has sometimes a Lax—which as a Medical Man I think a favourable circumstance an outlet to discharge what is Offensive to Nature, and if confined would fall on the Organs of respiration or some Vital Part————

Pray write Often you shall hear from me soon I wrote very lately————
Vale————

August 2 1769.

C

Letter from America expressing Anti-British feelings. 1770.

Dear Den,

The waggon harness together with your letter came safe to hand. Virginia is now determined to punish you for your crimes and are come to a resolution to have only such goods from England as they cannot live without; till the laws imposing taxes on us are repealed we shall be dressed in our own clothing, silks and all finery are not permitted to be landed here. Your merchants in England will feel the weight of resentment and curse the folly of your great politicians, you compel us to be frugal contrary to our natural inclination, in attempting to make us slaves you teach (us) to be independent, you send your troops here to break the peace & treat us as rebels when you yourselves are the cause of all disputes.

Mr Fairfax is drinking our medical waters he has been indisposed, an impostume has broke under his arm which will prove Saturday. He is expected here next month. Phill was well in June since which I have not heard from him, I wrote him lately—I must write to A . . ., soon, I shall only add that I . . .

am your affect . . .
(Bryan Martin)
Aug 15. 1770.

Questions

1. Do you think Bryan and Philip Martin are on the same side? Explain your answer fully by referring to their letters.
2. Bryan says, 'Politics daily gives rise to our disputes, tho' not the real cause' (B). What was the real cause?
3. Why could the English Taylor get away with selling bad cloths to the Virginians? (B). What did they do about this ultimately? (C).
4. Why did the colonists regard the Stamp Act as 'a load under which they were likely to sink'? (A).
5. What does Philip imply will happen if something isn't done about the Stamp Act? (A).
6. What do Bryan's 2 letters tell you about communications between Britain and America? Why might this be important in the struggle between them?
7. As Bryan hadn't heard from Philip since June (C), what might have happened to him.
8. Do you think the English were 'the cause of all disputes'? (C). Write a letter of reply from Den (Bryan's brother in England), putting the English point of view.

D

Letter from Bryan Martin to his Mother Oct. 31st 1765.

Dear Madam,

A gentleman lately arrived from Kent is with me, he calls me Brother but I know him not, had I met him I should have past him unnoticed, how I shall part with him is the question, the pleasure of meeting will not repay me for the pain in parting, how strange an alteration has fifteen years absence made, & how unexpected is our meeting, I gaze on him till lost in thought; let us forget past scenes & look forward the day must come that will make all things easey.

We divert ourselves with our Guns & ramble through Woods & Mountains Phill seems pleased with my situation it exceeded his Expectation, he grumbles at my Dress & says I am Mad, my Coat too long; my Hatt not fashionable, my stockings of an Improper Colour, nothing right.

Phills account of Affairs at Loose gives me pleasure, I shall remind the B—— of continuing his favours when ever an Opportunity offers, continue Corresponding with him even if he should not comply with your request just at the time you Expect it, he is. Slow in his Motions & teased for Cash by others. He who expects to live in this World free from trouble deceives himself, tho you have cause to complain of the unequall distribution of the Necessarys of this Life, yet are you happy in possessing more Valluable Blessings, take a view of your Children & you must be happy; not one that you can wish to disown.

This letter I send under Cover to Athaws, Phill is well and joyns me in his Duty . . . .

I am Mad^m what I ought to be
B———

EXTRACT 2

Punishments

On last Monday at the whipping post at Bishops Gate a vagrant ~ WILLIAM HALLET ~ was whipped barebacked, before being sent back to his place of origin, which is in Essex.

On last Friday at the Pillory at Ludgate a blasphemer, "Henry Wenthorpe" was sentenced to four hours in the said stocks. The local apprentices pelted him with various missiles.

On Monday at Newgate a man called Edward Globart, had his right hand cut off and was then hanged in the early hours of the morning, for attacking a fellow sailor in London Docks and clubbing him to death.

On last Monday at Westminster a man ~ Geoffrey Smett was sentenced to three hours in the pillory, for appearing drunk on the Sunday after celebrating all the previous night, and encouraging children to participate in a rowdy game and thus greatly disturbing the peace of the sabbath.

In the court of Star Chamber yesterday, Henry de Gray was fined £1,000 for harbouring Roman Catholic priests in a secret chamber and allowing, Mass to be held in his Manor well knowing the laws that our monarch hath made concerning the celebrating of Mass.

Carlos Hood

'WE've got you for history?' The emphasis of Graham's question was disquietingly on the 'you'. Graham was a member of a form which already, I had gathered, enjoyed the reputation of being about the most difficult to teach in the whole school. Both individually, and as a group, it embodied most of the problems of 'low-stream' classes. For a start, several of the form were barely literate, and thus required considerable help in quite simple tasks. An additional problem was the presence of a more than usually high number of children who were disturbed and who had troubled home backgrounds.

Graham himself was a very amiable boy, as, indeed, were almost all of his class-mates. As individuals, chatting at the end of the lesson or in the playgound, they were friendly enough. One felt that teachers were not disliked because of themselves so much, but because of what they forced the class to do during lesson-time.

Before giving a more detailed description of 3/7, one should first perhaps explain the organisation of my new school, and the area from which the school drew its intake. When I joined it, years three to six represented the secondary-modern intake, while the first two years were fully comprehensive in ability. Co-educational, like Thomas Bennett, it had a wider social range of pupils. The town had grown slowly since the coming of the railway, and was still semi-rural in character. A large proportion of the population were living on London 'overspill' council housing estates and, like Crawley, were first-generation families, although generally less prosperous. A good number of children came from surrounding villages and farms. Since the war there had been the growth of private housing estates in and around the town. The intake of the school was thus extremely heterogeneous in both social background and ability.

Within the school, the first two years were divided into two ability bands, with a considerable overlap of average-ability children. The pupils who had been there before it became a Comprehensive were divided into nine 'streams', although, particularly in the fourth year, there was a tendency to group streams together in optional subjects. About half the fourth year stayed on into the fifth and there was a sixth form of about forty, which included a small number of students taking subjects to 'A' level.

The history syllabus was a traditional one, except for a mode-three C.S.E. course. One had complete freedom, however, to develop one's own approach to a topic, and there was no pressure to 'cover' all the suggested items on the syllabus. In this, one was aided by the non-existence of exams in the first three years.

Although the partial non-streaming in the first two years did not solve all problems, it was a marked improvement on the system which operated in the third year upwards. In low-stream forms such as 3/7, most of the children had already 'given up' school; one or two had almost 'given up' themselves. An example of one of the latter was John. The wildness of John's behaviour and appearance made him rather an isolate, but normally he did have at least two mates: Terry and Derek. The effect of their going around together was mutually disastrous. Terry was inclined to truancy; his mother had left the family. Derek's father was so unco-operative that the Child Care Officer advised against further attempts by the school to contact the home; one of Derek's brothers had been in trouble with the police, and a general anti-authority attitude definitely had been fostered by the family. Terry required remedial help, while Derek, however, was of at least average intelligence. An 'under-achiever', in the second term he was in fact moved up a class, but this had no effect on his performance. Derek had decided to enter the Merchant Navy on leaving school, as one of his brothers had done; having come to the opinion that there was nothing in school which he either required or interested him, his sole aim was to have an easy time, occasionally stirring up others to make trouble.

If in this triumvirate Derek was the leader, Terry, and particularly John, were the led. John was easily one of the most difficult boys in the school; yet at times he could be likeable. He required great patience and a good deal of help. He came from a large, none too well-off family, whose mother found the task of managing the home difficult. This, however, was not a sufficient reason for John's behaviour, as none of his brothers and sisters posed the same problems. As is usually the case, the history of his clashes with authority began at Primary School; aged nine he had already been referred to the Educational Psychologist, when a lack of security in his family had been suggested as the reason for his uncontrolled and violent behaviour. This may have been so. Certainly backwardness and the loss of sight in one eye did not encourage the growth of self-confidence. Now in his early 'teens, John was generally aggressive towards both staff and fellow pupils; every opportunity was used to make his presence felt.

John's demands for praise were as frequent as his violent outbursts; to an extent the one stemmed from the lack of the other. The feelings of inferiority which this reflected were not confined to John. Not surprisingly, when one knows their histories, virtually all of 3/7 needed continuous reassurance that they were succeeding and that their efforts were of value; their position in the streamed situation alone would have guaranteed this. One could rely on Neal, for example, who had known three fathers and spent some time in a special school as a result of asthma, always to make a fuss lasting at least five minutes before he got down to work; work which he was quite capable of tackling adequately. Unfortunately, it was not until towards the end of the year that one began to understand the reasons for Neal acting the way he did. Largely as a result of a joint interest in school football, I got to know Neal fairly well. His comment on gaining a place at a local Technical College was that 'You don't have to be upper-class to go to college', which reflected the feelings of educational inadequacy under which Neal and a good number of others laboured. Nicola, who had her ambitions firmly fixed on Woolworth's, would make a similar fuss about settling down to work. Peter would preface every lesson with the question, 'When are we going to do aircraft?'. After all, planes were one of the few topics that he felt he knew anything about.

It was some time before one began to acquire the necessary detailed awareness about each member of the form. Moreover, one's first lesson had gone deceptively well. At the end of it several had discussed their summer holidays; John graphically described his adventures at a Scout camp. Shortly, however, one's lessons became more arduous. The first crisis erupted at a part of a lesson when most were working quietly. John, pushed from behind, turned and shouted at Richard, the boy responsible, to 'Fuck off'. It might have been better if I had punished him straight away. Instead I told him to see me at the end of the lesson, and discussed with him the rights and wrongs of swearing when a lot of people were present. Although John did swear several other times in my presence, he never did so again so that the whole class would hear. This particular instance of 'bad' behaviour typified the sort of uncontrolled reaction by children such as John with which one met so frequently in 3/7. There was the associated problem of what one's own response should be. A quiet, reasoned approach would seem more likely to induce similar behaviour. On the other hand, the instinctive reaction was to take a more decisive line; the only teachers 3/7 always obeyed were those ones who were prepared, albeit sparingly, to inflict some form of physical punishment.

Meanwhile, one relied on preparation, 'ringing the changes' as regards topic and method and, not least, on persuasion and a sense of humour. One was usually able to have worksheets ready, or work set out on the blackboard. One used contemporary accounts, even, on a couple of occasions, attempted acting in groups, but rarely could the co-operation of everyone in the class be induced at the same time. Indeed it seemed at times as if they took it in turns to be a nuisance. When John or Richard were quiet, then more likely than not one or more of the girls would prove awkward.

The period when relations with 3/7 were at their best was in the half-term before Christmas. It was at this time that they worked on a topic of their own choice. I had intended that it be a subject from the eighteenth or early nineteenth centuries, as this was the period we were currently doing work on, but the area of choice was soon forced much wider. John, for example, chose to study aircraft, which meant that at the start of one lesson soon after, I was presented by him with several pages of a scrap-book filled, in no particular pattern, with several pages of cigarette-packet pictures of aircraft, all displaying evidence of an over-liberal use of glue. After having said the right words of encouragement, I then tried to get him to copy a picture of a plane from one of the library books I had brought in. During the course of the lesson he attempted the drawing three times, on each occasion tearing the paper up, as 'Not good enough'. Nonetheless, most of the class managed to work reasonably well and some quite good projects resulted. It was fortunate for me that it was at this time that the Deputy Head, who was responsible for supervising me in my probationary year, chose to sit in on a lesson.

At no time, however, were they an easy group to teach. Attempts at imaginative writing were bedevilled by their low level of literacy, and a general reluctance to tackle anything beyond their known experience. Occasionally one of the class produced a passage of writing which showed a certain life (see Extract 1 at end of this section), but generally they found work of this sort difficult. Discussion was more often than not wrecked by disputes between members of the form. With so high a proportion of disturbed children in the group, one of the main problems was to moderate the inter-pupil hostilities.

Even project work, when introduced a second time, failed to

arouse much interest. A project on 'War' had developed out of the showing of the film *Culloden*. There was brief, initial enthusiasm; John, who had given up the Scouts for the A.C.F. and now expressed a wish to enter the Army, brought in a shell-case and I got him to tell the rest of the class where he had found it. Another boy came in a few weeks later with a German helmet. The novelty effect of all this, however, soon wore off.

For several reasons, one generally felt that all one did was not only superficial, but superfluous. It was rather like forcing a ward of chronically sick patients to discuss the Common Market. How could Susan concentrate on anything at school with a home situation which included a mother who, when not deserting the home, was attempting suicide? Even with those who came from more settled backgrounds, their resistance to class-work, which their sense of failure and apathy induced, proved too great a barrier to break down. Nothing, for example, would reconcile David, one of the noisier boys, to not having been promoted at the end of the first year when he believed he ought to have been. (When he did go up three streams at the end of the year his work and attitude changed considerably and he stayed on into the fifth.) Richard, during one of several long conversations we had when I was on playground duty, openly admitted to 'being a bugger in class' because he felt that, for him, school was a waste of time.

Out of the class-room most were not only friendly but also responsible. Indeed the nature of many of their home backgrounds forced them to grow up very early. When a party of third-formers were taken to Portsmouth to visit H.M.S. *Victory*, the girls from 3/7 were noticeably more sensible than some of those from classes above them. It was ironic, but significant, that their worst behaviour was reserved for the class-room.

In my first year about half of my time-table was with the mixed-ability groups and they provided quite a contrast with 3/7. The wide range of ability obviously posed its own problems, but the resistance to school work which characterised Derek, John, Susan and colleagues was much less in evidence. Especially among the groups made up of the average and below average-ability children there were certainly one or two in each class who were finding school difficult and not normally too enjoyable. In the third year a small number of such children did cause the same problems as those posed by the majority of the children in the low-stream classes. In almost every case, however, although themselves reacting against school, their behaviour did not make the remainder of the group unteachable. On the positive side there were several examples of children who under the former system would have been in the seventh, eighth, or ninth stream, but because they were in a group whose attitude to school was much less negative, both their standard and attitude to work improved. Whereas little had been achieved of whom little had been expected, now many far-from-able children had a much better chance of taking part in activities, such as visits and plays in which previously staff would have been dubious about allowing them to participate.

It had already been intended that children should spend much more of their time on topic work of their own choice and the need for this, in order to arouse and maintain interest in the subject, was reinforced by the nature of mixed-ability teaching. Even if one had wished to retain the emphasis on traditional class-room teaching, the wide variation in the speed with which children worked would have forced second thoughts. The necessity of re-thinking teaching techniques became that much greater in the third year when history classes often included children from both extremes of the intelligence scale.

On several grounds, therefore, individualised learning would have to take up a considerable section of the time. To adopt a Primary School-style approach to learning in the framework of a Secondary School day, posed several problems, however. Lessons were often in different rooms, books had to be carried a considerable distance around the school. Quite frequently when one arrived at the class-room, the teacher's desk was the only place that could be used to put the different sets of books, drawing and writing paper, magazines, pictures, the library books on project loan, and all the other items that one required when a class was working on a project. Apart from the single history room, there was rarely storage space for either materials or children's incomplete work. With periods of thirty-five or forty minutes, beginning work, and then clearing away, often took about half the lesson. With time at a premium in every lesson, organisation of each individual's work beforehand was obviously essential. Several chaotic sessions early on underlined this, and subsequently one or more lessons were spent before a project commenced, finding out which particular task or topic the children wished to work on, how they would work —alone, in pairs, or small groups, and in explaining where paper, books, and so on would be found, and how books and other source material were to be borrowed. Duplicated sheets with page and picture references, together with suggestions for different types of work, would be handed out. Only then would each child begin its project. In classes with a few non-readers, there was still the problem of how to get detailed instructions across, and this could only be done verbally, a little at a time. Provided the work had been sufficiently organised the majority would not now take long to settle down, and one then could go quickly to those who had to be told individually what to do.

The children were normally given a complete choice as to how they would work. Usually they would do so in pairs, and not uncommonly this allowed a non-reader to team up with a more capable child. It was noticeable how 'brighter' children often volunteered to assist the less able, by reading a work-sheet for them, getting books, and occasionally asking me questions when the other child was very shy. This co-operation I encouraged, as it was of help to me as well as to the children involved, and I cannot recall a case of the less able hampering the more able as a result.

Although project work was popular and produced a high standard of work, some problems still remain. Ensuring that all the class gained from the researches of each child is very difficult; most children are not particularly successful at giving a résumé of what they have found. There is also the tendency for the less able to do little more than copy, even when a question has been so framed as to make it impossible to answer correctly by so doing. At the very least, however, interest and motivation were greater than probably would have been the case with formal teaching, and individual work allowed each child to work at his own speed and not at a hypothetical common speed guessed at by the teacher.

Work-sheets were also useful when work on a particular book or topic was being set, as a wide range of tasks could be incorporated. Setting the work was merely a matter of distributing the sheets, and consequently there was more time to see each pupil.

Although work-sheets are suited to mixed-ability classes, children are not suited to an unrelieved diet of work-sheets. One of the advantages of history teaching is that there is a fairly wide range of activities and sources which one can use. One approach that I thought especially worth trying was the use of original prose and poetry to introduce a period to a class. On teaching practice I had read extracts from the tenth-century English poem, *The Battle of Maldon*, with a top-stream first-year class. In my first year at my new school I had been pleased with the way in which fairly lengthy sections from the Rosemary Sutcliff translation of *Beowulf* had been received. The class in question contained several non-readers, and so I had merely read from my copy, and yet their attention had been held for the whole lesson, and obviously this was one of the few pieces of work that all the class remembered and enjoyed.

Consequently, the following year I decided to build up a whole term's work from the reading of original Anglo-Saxon prose and poetry, in translation. The most important source was to be *Beowulf*, but as well, extracts from Bede and the *Anglo-Saxon Chronicle*, as well as long sections from *The Battle of Maldon*. This work was done in co-operation with the English department, and it was they who purchased the set of *Beowulf*. During the two periods of English set aside for this work, the extracts of poetry would be read and discussed as such. Drama and imaginative writing would develop from what was read. In the history lessons, the poems and stories would be treated as source material in an attempt to get the children to see how historical literature is one source of information about the past, and how it links up with other means of enquiry, such as archaeology. When, for example, in *The Battle of Maldon*, one of Brihtnoth's thegns declares,

> I swear that from this spot not one foot's space
> Of ground shall I give up. I shall go onwards,
> In the fight avenge my friend and lord.
> My deeds shall give no warrant for words of blame
> to steadfast men on the Stour, now he is stretched lifeless,
> —that I left the battle field a lordless man,
> turned for home . . .'

the Saxon ethic of loyalty and dependence to one's lord are vividly expressed.

When the children had learned as much as possible about the Saxon or Viking way of life, they would then follow up their interests by project work in the usual way. Supplementing the literature, the other sources of information, such as place-name evidence and archaeological finds, were discussed. I had been lucky to have had three weeks' digging at South Cadbury, in Somerset, and my own descriptions and photographs, together with news-paper pictures and cuttings, provided a basis for a comparison of the fictitious Arthur and the historical figure of the late-fifth and early sixth centuries. The Sutton Hoo treasure was used as another example of how archaeological and literary evidence complemented each other. A visit to see the Sutton Hoo discoveries in the British Museum played a useful part in the individual work the children were doing.

Every fortnight or so there would be a joint English and history homework. This took the form of a piece of imaginative writing based on an extract they had been reading. The English teacher would spend plenty of time explaining what was wanted, and this included historical accuracy. The homework would then be marked by both of us, with my colleague concentrating on the work as a piece of English and myself paying most attention to its merits as a reasonably correct description of what it was supposed to portray.

The form concerned in this work was one from the second of the two ability bands and which, by chance, contained one of the widest ranges of ability. One lad, Ian, had a very good general knowledge and I had only to mention a book in the library for him to borrow it and read it. At the other end of the scale there were five children who were definitely backward and who were badly lacking in confidence. Priscilla, for example, was terribly withdrawn and had a reading-age of 5·2 when she entered the school. So as to ensure that the non-readers missed nothing, the extracts were read aloud, with frequent pauses for questions and comments and it was clear that all the class were able to follow the story. Difficult vocabulary was dealt with similarly.

The main aim of the term's work was to get across the idea of how we know about the past, and the correlating of one form of evidence with another. Such a scheme would perhaps appear at first sight to be unrealistic, particularly with a group of below-average intelligence. However, class and individual discussion, written work and tests showed that, with the exception of Priscilla, the points one had hoped to make had got across. Likewise, the concept of historical anachronism is a fairly sophisticated one, yet the imaginative work produced for homework avoided the more obvious examples of anachronistic writing. A high proportion of the stories, poems and plays the children were asked to write were vivid pieces of work (see Extract 2).

For Priscilla and the others like her in 1B/2, it was an achievement even to write a sentence, and although they were encouraged to manage as much as possible, written homework had to be supplemented by the drawing of simple pictures or diagrams to illustrate the story. Andrew, whose reading age was 6·3 at the beginning of the year, was one of these children, yet to observe his keenness to take part in the discussion of a film or film-strip, no one would suspect that he needed remedial help. As good chance would have it, 1B/2 were a particularly pleasant class and Andrew's keenness to participate fully in the lesson was a general characteristic of the group. Even allowing for this, one was sufficiently encouraged to plan work of a similar nature for the subsequent year.

Beowulf and the other original material obviously lent themselves to drama work, and a considerable amount of classroom acting was done. Whether a fairly involved piece of acting or not, classroom drama presented several good opportunities. As a means of telling a story it had a much greater impact on the children than merely reading it. It gave extrovert and imaginative alike the chance to shine, and gave everyone a break from more passive activities.

In my first year the History Department had agreed to put on a History Evening which would include the dramatisation of various events from the syllabus of the first two years. I chose to do my contribution with 2W/2. There were several quite capable actors in the class, and a playlet lasting about ten minutes presented few problems. Several times in the autumn term I had had them divide into groups and prepare a brief play based on the topic we had been studying. It normally took a period for them to sort out who was to play each character and to write a brief script. I found this degree of preparation necessary, as only a few children were able to make up the lines as they went along. Then either a homework period, or some time in a subsequent period, was allowed for the learning of lines. The children normally liked a 'run-through' and if, as occasionally happened, neighbouring class-rooms were empty, these, together with corridors, could be used for a brief rehearsal.

2W/2 contained several children who still were receiving remedial teaching. One girl, Coral, was also partially deaf and very withdrawn, and would not normally take part in the dramatised scenes. Boys such as Frank and Derek, both of whom had difficulty in expressing themselves on paper, were full of ideas when it came to acting. Frank was one of the few in the class who could improvise, and I remember well a scene between him, as Henry VIII, and Jim, playing the part of Thomas More. Jim, unlike Frank, could write as well as he could act, but an outsider would not have been able to say which of the two was the boy who needed remedial help. Something which virtually all the class were able to do was the production of props. Often they were simple objects such as cardboard swords with silver paper wrapped around them, but this similarly allowed the whole range of ability to work co-operatively, but yet not to the detriment of any other child.

The side-benefits of combining action and history were obvious when it came to the History Evening. By setting it in an imaginary Elizabethan market-place it was possible to include all the form. I duplicated the outline of the play, with the children adding ideas of their own. Costumes and props were kept simple, and the children had no difficulty in learning their lines, which, in any case, were few enough. Up to a certain point it was possible to

E

rehearse during normal lesson time. Rehearsals using the stage could only be arranged after school. This raised problems as a good number of the children had to catch coaches to quite distant villages, and at this time I rather regretted including the whole class in the production. On the night, however, apart from Jim accidentally knocking the pillory over, an incident which was calmly ignored by the children, everything went smoothly. Once safely over, I was glad I had included everybody in the play. There was considerable satisfaction in seeing children such as Coral on the stage. Admittedly she had not said anything, but she was involved in what the remainder of the class were doing and had managed something many people would have thought unlikely. In comparison with other school productions, 'A Tudor Market Scene' was very small fry, yet the mingled pride and pleasure which members of 2W/2 still talked of the play some twelve months later, in my view gave it a great deal of value.

Similar in its merits to acting is the use of the tape-recorder. A tape-recorded series of imaginary interviews, for example, is a different and, particularly in a class where there are several remedial children, useful method of testing to what extent a topic has been assimilated. In my second year I was fortunate that one of my third-form groups was very small—fourteen in all. They were not an especially academic group; about half later went on to follow a C.S.E. course. One boy, Nigel, was still receiving remedial tuition and he had rather a reputation as a trouble-maker. Another, Derek, was a rotund, easy-going lad from a gypsy family, whose speed working in class was as slow as his movement around the school. In a low-stream form these and one or two of the other boys might have been quite difficult to control. As it was, they still needed fairly close watching and pressure over such things as homework, but there was none of the antagonism that one met with from some boys in 3/7.

Given the nature of the class, I did a fair amount of work using a tape-recorder. A story we read about smuggling was turned into a taped-play, and if as much enthusiasm was put into getting the correct number of owl-hoots and the sound of approaching horses as the spoken parts, this did not detract from the completed tape. Later on in the year the class split into two groups and we taped imaginary interviews with sailors who had been at Trafalgar. Some of the more enthusiastic boys then asked if we could tape a scene involving a Press Gang, and this was done without any preparation at all. I remember this occasion well as Nigel's enthusiastic practising of swinging open the class-room door, to get the sound of the inn-door being burst open, led to some suspicious glances by the Deputy Head who was passing at the time.

There was another example of a virtually unrehearsed taping, after I had told the same class a local story concerning the navvies and the building of the local railway. It took the form of a drama-tisation of the clash between a group of Irish and a group of Scottish navvies outside a pub. All the accents were surprisingly good and this tape ended on a fade-out of 'Irish Eyes Are Smiling'. Nigel in particular identified himself with this particular story and, together with the others, even stayed through some of the break to finish, losing some of his precious 'fag-time' to do so!

With 3/7 only once had I used a tape-recorder. It had been as part of work based on a contemporary account of a smuggling incident, which I had taken from the archive kit on eighteenth-century smuggling produced by the East Sussex Record Office. The story was dramatic enough, but even with a few modifications in wording, it still proved too difficult for most of 3/7, who, as usual, were not prepared to make any effort to follow something which they did not find immediately comprehensible. Connected with the description of the ambush of a group of smugglers by Preventive Officers was a letter written by one of the witnesses to the subsequent trial. After we had read both the account of the ambush and the letter, I attempted to get the class to work out answers to questions which I set.

After the possible answers had been discussed, the topic was then completed by attempting to dramatise the whole story, using the tape-recorder. When it came to this, 3/7 made a little more effort, but even this was not particularly successful as most of the groups merely repeated the story, whereas I had hoped that they would make up an ending to it. With a more able third-year group the response to this particular piece of work had been better. Some still found the comprehension work beyond them, but there were suffi-cient children in the class who were able enough to put forward sensible answers to get a discussion going about the sort of informa-tion that could be reasonably deduced from the account; I was even able to make the point that different conclusions may be equally valid and that this is one of the factors that a historian has to accept.

Work on similar lines with second-year classes likewise varied in its success. For example, based on an article in one of the Sunday colour supplements, I duplicated sheets with the information. We then read these, considering whether or not, seeing that it came from Government sources, the evidence was at all suspect. Between them, the children saw all the dubious points in the Government story that I hoped they would, but again there was a few in the class who obviously had not been able to follow what the remainder had been saying. Most of the children enjoyed this detective-style type of work, and subsequently there was a spate of questions as to the validity of other historical accounts.

The work on the smuggling story and the Gunpowder Plot, together with some of the first-year work already described, were all attempts at a 'Fenton-style' approach to history teaching (see Section 4). From looking at duplicated, and sometimes rephrased accounts, the next step was to make a study of photocopies of original documents. The relevant sheets of the 1861 Census for the neighbouring village were duly photocopied. While other members of the department used them with some fourth and fifth form groups, I tried using them with a Local History group I had on Thursday afternoons. Some of the writing was none too easy to read, and several pages were badly obscured as is often the case with Census material. However, a quite cursory study of their contents, looking at size of families and so on, was quite within the capabilities of a mixed-ability group of first and second-year children. As well as house and street names, the names of several families were known to some of the group, and this naturally helped to stimulate interest. Work on original sources need not be confined to written material. In the visits we made to surrounding villages and towns, questions about the particular route of a prehistoric trackway, the location of a church or house, or why archaeologists chose one place to excavate from a Roman villa rather than another, all required the children to think historically.

One's experience with attempts at 'Fenton'-work had not been too discouraging, although work on these lines had been very tentative, and interspersed with more mundane activities. One was still far from successfully meeting the challenge that this type of work met when one taught mixed-ability classes, but it was quite possible to keep the whole class involved, providing that one did not always insist on every child producing work which was written. And a wide range of tasks presupposed a similarly wide range of resources for the children to use.

Although, for example, in 1B/2 Andrew had enjoyed and understood the passages we had read from *Beowulf*, *The Battle of Maldon*, etc., Nigel, in 3B/D was completely lost when I asked him to answer the questions on the smuggling extracts. It was difficult to know how far the problem was lack of confidence, as with Neal in 3/7, or that one was asking something of which he at this stage was not capable. To what extent was it the subject-matter? An issue which he felt more interest in may well have led to more success. As the problem of how to introduce material so that all individuals in the form could come to grips with it successfully had not yet been solved, so also the question of what the syllabus should be remained. In the partially un-streamed situation the opposition to school which had characterised classes such as 3/7 was confined to no more than one or two individuals. On the other hand, apathy and hostility had not been banished with the streaming. The reasons for such attitudes, like the solutions, were various and could only be resolved by more than one agency. What the school offered, however, obviously is important, and although I found that as a history teacher the popularity of the subject, which was pretty general lower down in the school, certainly did not disappear in the third year, complaints about its use and relevance were met with. New approaches to a subject may not be sufficient by themselves.

To be relevant, of course, one has not necessarily to scrap teaching the past. One of the most rewarding topics in our third-form syllabus, for example, was the story of the 1745 Jacobite rising. As part of the work on it we showed the film *Culloden* with all the three groups in the third year that I taught last year, and the film made exactly the impression one had hoped. The children had grasped most of the points that Peter Watkins had made in the film. Although it is said that it is virtually impossible to have an adult discussion in a totally mixed-ability class, all the children took part in discussing the historical and moral points which the film raised. On their own initiative at least one member of each class compared the outrages after Culloden with those in Vietnam. The film was shown shortly after the My Lai incident, and discussion of Cumberland's behaviour quickly passed on to the consideration of wartime atrocities generally. The effect of the film had obviously been a deep one, and this came out in some of the written work which follows. Some of the most effective pieces of work were poems (see Extract 3).

The belated introduction of Primary School techniques into the teaching of history to older children was originally the result of fear about the health of the subject. With the gradual but inevitable introduction of mixed-ability classes (teaching in the first year is completely mixed ability this year), this process will be virtually mandatory if non-streaming is to show itself superior to the system it replaces. Emphasis must be on active involvement, with a wide range of visits, documentary and other original material, L.P. records, films and slides, and other visual material, all forming a multi-media impetus resource for children's work, which to a large extent will be individually programmed. This in turn will force changes in the school day; thirty-five minute periods in three different rooms a week, most of which lack adequate storage or display space, are clearly anachronistic. Much more combined and integrated teaching is also obviously required. One's own small-scale experience with 1B/2 shows the value of teachers combining on similar work. Not least, pooled knowledge about children is even more useful when one is dealing with the total ability range. Deciding upon what basis assessment of children can be done is merely one of the problems that a wide range of abilities highlights.

At the end of two years' teaching, most of which, apart from one's time with classes preparing for exams, had been spent with mixed-ability classes, I was still far from solving the problems these classes, or, for that matter, teaching in general, posed. On the other hand, if I was still concerned that there were times when the least able were not being aided sufficiently, I had seen little signs that the most able were suffering from the break with streaming. And whereas, with 3/7, the nature of the class had largely thwarted attempts to make the subject more interesting and worthwhile, the generally more positive atmosphere in classes who had not suffered from a system of rigid streaming, meant that changes in method could be given a fair trial. With 3/7 one had been pleased, and not a little surprised, to find that the children were far from unlikeable. In the mixed-ability groups, not only were the children equally likeable, but there was also a genuine liking for history. With the changes in school organisation and teaching techniques there is perhaps a good chance that this interest will be strengthened in school, rather than, as so often in the past, surviving *in spite of* school history or—more common still—disappearing for good.

EXTRACT 1

Life in the Navy at the Time of Nelson

Dear mum

I feel impelled to write this letter because I want you to know what it is like in the navy. The cabin boy stole $4\frac{1}{2}$d from the coxwain and then received 1 dozen lashes with salt and vinegar put on every ½ dozen that was yesterday, today A man was hung for telling the captain to 'get stuffed' and a bit more becides. What ever you do dont let Willie join I feel envieous of him in lovely comfotable cell in the scrubs. And the food, dish out any more and they will soon be having us eating the spare sails.

Yours
Fred.

Remember

Remember what we said,
Remember?
We'll be so brave we said,
Remember?
We told the women folk how brave we'll be,
Remember?
And they laughed,
Remember?
Nobody wants to go to war they said,
Remember?

Remember what we told them,
Remember?
We'll be so brave that they will run when they see us,
Remember?
Remember what they said,
Remember?
Expect you will run,
But if you do, don't come back to us.

Remember that? Now look at us,
Running, running from the war.
There, there lay men dead,
But at least they fought with their King
And are not disgraced.
But we have no one to go to,
Remember?
Remember we have no one to go to.

DENISE NEWMAN

EXTRACT 3

Culloden

Grey is the day
The day of death
We'll follow Charlie
And die!

Grey are our hearts
The hearts of heroes
Yes, the cold heroes
Of Inverness!

Sun coming up
It smiles at our blood
Scottish blood,
Red blood!

It's over now
The battle, but
Where is Charlie?
He's gone.

Not a word of thanks,
Never a word,
He's gone.
And left the cold heroes
of Inverness.

*   *   *

Chris Culpin

As I came to the University of Sussex, and to Thomas Bennett School, Crawley, a year after Pat Kendell and Carlos Hood, and have only been teaching for one year, I remember very clearly what it felt like to cope for the first time with teaching in a Comprehensive School. Having spent the previous eighteen months away from teaching and, prior to that, a pleasant, sheltered year teaching the sixth form of a boys' Grammar School, I was somewhat apprehensive at the prospect. How on earth did you teach non-academic children? And girls? In a school three times the size of any I had ever known?

'Spend today sitting in on lessons', said John Townsend. 'You needn't start teaching until tomorrow.' Tomorrow!

Tomorrow's lesson was with a first-year class and I was to teach them about Iron Age hill-forts, so I spent several hours the evening before reading and preparing. The lesson came, I talked throughout the time, forgot to show the pictures I had found, and drew a scrappy and misleading diagram on the blackboard. In addition, I alienated a girl near the front of the class by telling her, rather sharply, not to interrupt me, and she sulked, pointedly, for the rest of the lesson. The next day they had forgotten almost all of what I had said.

However, I appeared to have been accepted as their history teacher and received cheerful greetings along the corridors, which gave me confidence and encouragement to pay more attention to the children and less to my material alone. I also quickly appreciated the sure observation and sound advice John Townsend offered to me. Often, merely to put into words in my lesson-reaction notes for him, the frustration a lesson had caused, helped me to find the source of a problem for myself. It was, particularly, the details of technique in getting on easy terms with the children that I was grateful to pick up. For the sulking first-year girl of my first lesson, John suggested that I single her out for a casual and quick word of praise at the beginning of the next lesson, while handing out the books. I did, she grinned, and we were friends for the rest of the time I taught her.

Of course, not all problems were solved as easily, or links made with children so quickly, but it had been rapidly brought home to me that my first concern must be to build up a good relationship with the class, and with the individuals in it. At Thomas Bennett, because of the University of Sussex system of teaching practice throughout the year, I was enabled to spend time doing this, picking up on my mistakes and trying to get over them by my own efforts, over a lengthy period of time. There is no substitute for experience here, but any short-cuts and insights gained along the way are invaluable, and it is the young teacher who is probably most in need of help in coping with the personal problems involved in teaching, and who is obviously shortest on experience. I was very glad of what skill of this nature I had managed to acquire when my lesson planning broke down once or twice during the stresses and strains of my first year. 'Don't worry, sir, we're all students here', as one of the fourth-year boys at Thomas Bennett put it. On the positive side, once an easy working relationship has been built up then the range of possible approaches in teaching, and the readiness to experiment, are all greatly increased by the confidence teacher and pupils have in each other.

With this priority in mind, together with one or two aims about history teaching, and a few lessons up my sleeve, I prepared for my first year as a full-time teacher in a Comprehensive School. One of the classes to test me out most during the next year was a second-year group. We got off to a rather shaky start as I had been led to expect a mixed-ability group, when in fact they were a bottom-English set, put together for history for some administratively convenient reason. The syllabus was a thematic one centred on man and religion, starting with myths and legends. It would have been quite simple to have given out the names and attributes of the Greek gods, and told a few stories about them, but that would not have been of great value, except as information, which would be rapidly forgotten. I wanted to try and get across the meaning of a system of many gods to a primitive society, and to enable the children to devise this, and, in some way, experience this, for themselves. We, therefore, spent a lesson on ghost stories and possible explanations for them, and then in the next lesson I asked them all to pretend that we were on an island in the Pacific; we talked of the things we would need for a comfortable, if primitive, life and appointed a ruler (the biggest boy), and a queen (the prettiest girl). I then said that the important job of witch-doctor would go to the person who could offer the most convincing explanations for various natural phenomena; rain, tides, thunder, lightning, etc. When the answers were read out I was delighted to find that a god or gods were mentioned. We discussed the meaning of this, and elected our witch-doctor.

During the lessons, which I suppose were not really history at all, I was able to talk to individual children about their ideas, and so begin to know them, and to talk to the whole group, so that they could know me. Individuals emerged very quickly: Alec, who was full of ideas, bounced about calling for attention, but could hardly write; Gary who could draw beautifully but was sullen and resentful if pushed into writing; and Christine, who tried hard, but was very shy and lacking in imagination. The group contained seven children classed as remedial, four of whom could not really read or write without great difficulty. Several of the children were regularly in trouble, inside and outside school, and there were only six girls in the whole class, as girls tend to be brighter at that age. In general they seemed less imaginative than the Crawley children of the previous year: the rural catchment area of the school and its position in south-west England probably contributed to this. Christine, for example, as I learnt later, lived alone on a farm with her parents, and only saw other children at school or at church. She had never been to the nearest city, ten miles away.

I was determined that I was not going to surrender to easy mindless tasks with this class, however, but to maintain valid history whenever possible. I had always scorned the history teachers of my past who produced crayons and pictures in order to avoid difficulties, and Ken Brown, from the remedial department of another Crawley school, had shown what worthwhile and interesting work children of this ability could tackle. Clearly they were not going to cope with a 'Fenton-type' kit, even if I had had the time or resources to prepare one, but it seems fair to ask that children make an imaginative response to a situation, and use their imagination and intelligence to solve problems. For our 'witch-doctor' problem, Alec suggested that an earthquake was 'a giant fish hitting the side of the island' and that thunder was 'the gods' conversation'. Someone else suggested that an eclipse was 'a god nibbling the moon'. When it came to the Greek gods, I presented each one as a member of a family and hoped that they could be understood as personalities. But with such difficulties in expressing themselves, how could the class show if they had picked up this almost intuitive sense of people's personalities? At this point, Gary had a birthday, and was telling me about his presents, and I decided to ask them to compile a list of gifts given by the Greek gods if they came to a party, each present to be in character. Even the non-writers could manage a word for each, and the criterion would be imaginativeness, not fluency. Among the suggestions were: Zeus—a rocket, Poseidon—a turtle, Hephaistos—a horseshoe, Ares—a medal, Demeter—a toy combine-harvester, Hermes—some foreign money and Hades—a skeleton.

Looking back on this, it seems a somewhat quirky exercise, with not a great deal of value, and not really very historical, except in a distant way, but it was a means of achieving some imaginative thought from everyone in the class, even if some answers were rather feeble. I can't really object to the anachronisms in their answers at this stage; provided they are not too glaringly obvious (like the washing-machine Christine's Pilgrim Father took with him later in the year) it can at least show that the child has an immediate link with a historical person, even if the details are awry.

Later in the year, I used the same idea of asking for an imaginative appreciation of character while using three of Chaucer's pilgrims as illustrations of relaxed standards in the Church in the late Middle Ages. Chaucer's descriptions of the Monk, the Prioress and the Friar are so modern and so effective in their irony that they provide an excellent lead to a wide variety of imaginative responses. Several of the girls began to write and perform little dramatic scenes about each of them, some drew and some wrote stories. (To be fair, some did very little at all and had to be talked into it.) I had got to know Gary much better by this stage, and was still trying to get him to write something for me, but had, so far, failed almost entirely. I knew his father kept a pub, and gathered that Gary liked his father and was fascinated by life in the Public Bar, where he occasionally helped with the washing-up. We talked about the three pilgrims, what they would drink, what their types might drink now, looked at Alec's pictures of them, and then he wrote this (spelling corrected):

> 'I was serving two regulars when these three strangers walked in. Said they were on the way to Canterbury. There was a monk. He looked quite well-off, and the stable-boy told me he was riding a huge grey mare, with brass studs along the bridle. He ordered best French wine and ate a whole leg of salted pork. The lady was a Prioress, dressed in fine silk robes, and she had a chicken, but ate only the breast. Half of that she gave to her little dogs. The other was a friar. He sat in the Saloon and chatted up the barmaids.'

I like this because he used the information he had, shuffled it around in his mind, and produced an imaginative response, which tells us far more about the characters than if he had merely been told: 'Describe the Monk, the Prioress and the Friar in your own words.' I also like it because it was the only piece he wrote for me in the year, apart from the most perfunctory efforts.

From the lessons described so far, it would appear that I was the focus of attention and sole source of information during the lesson in most cases, and that the class all worked together on tasks inspired, selected and controlled by me; in fact that was the case far too often during the year, largely because of the scarcity of resources available on the topics I was required to cover. More child-centred work needs plenty of resources, and these were not nearly so readily available as they had been at Thomas Bennett and the University of Sussex. The school had only become comprehensive the previous year, by amalgamating the local Grammar and Secondary Modern schools, and the books and other resources were still rather fragmentary. Given these circumstances, which I felt were unsatisfactory, and the fact that the theme of the syllabus was not as clear to my particular class as it might have been, I decided to spend some time in the summer term on what might be called a small 'patch'. I chose the Armada and the events of 1588 for this, and by accident stumbled on a topic which struck chords with many of the class: boats and sailing, the Navy and the south-west coast were the most important elements in the lives of many of the boys, and although there was not much in the way of close local ties, it was a topic that did, in the end, interest a great number of the class.

To start off, we went up to the cliff near the school and, looking out to sea, I went briefly over the story of the Armada. The cliff was also a beacon-point and we could point out the main beacons within range. Back at school, we all went swiftly through a standard textbook account and then the class split up into pairs or threes to cover parts of the story in individual projects. The range of interest here became very wide: Gary and a friend investigated the ships of the English Fleet, what they were like to sail, where they were supplied from, etc.; Christine was interested in life on board the ships, both English and Spanish; Alec and his friend covered tactics and the battle campaign; some did weapons and English home defences; others dealt with the beacon alarm system and traced the network all over southern England. The girls, it must be said, were not interested in all this, but undertook to write biographies of the chief sailors of the English Fleet, after I had pointed out that they ought to do something, and became gradually quite interested.

Having chosen subjects for investigation, everyone now wanted source material, and for some time I was kept busy scurrying round the groups trying to keep everyone happy. I severely underestimated what they would need, and before the next lesson had to raid several libraries to find suitable books and pictures. The Jackdaw on the Armada was quite helpful, but more than half the documents could only be glanced at, rescued by me from the floor and pinned on the wall, where they soon outlived their usefulness. One Jackdaw did not go very far, either, and in the end I found three of them only just stretched round the groups. Ordinary school textbooks for this level were soon rejected by the children as far too superficial, and I was driven on to the *Then and There* series on 'Plymouth Ho!' and even to Garrett Mattingly's book on the Spanish Armada. Provided the pages are pointed out beforehand

and help given with difficult words, there seems no real reason why such adult books cannot be used by children at almost any level. Reading was normally very reluctantly done, but given a real desire to find out, for example, exactly how a galleon tacked, the most complex books were used, just as the boy in Ken Loach's film *Kes* struggled through the book on falconry.

I had never gone deeply into the topic of the Armada either, so I greatly enjoyed the discoveries that the groups made. If I had covered the topic myself in a shorter time, two or three ortho-dox 'talk and chalk' lessons might have resulted, perhaps mildly interesting, but soon forgotten. With individuals making their own discoveries it was much more like a piece of genuine historical research. Fortunately, also, the topic enabled them to use their judgement and knowledge to balance conflicting opinions as the more detailed books provided opinions at variance with the usual story retold in the school textbooks. This was an added bonus that I had not expected, but was an invaluable exercise for them in drawing conclusions based on their own knowledge and experience, and cutting romantic yarns down to size.

Having described all this, however, I should be the first to reject the idea of trying this sort of project approach all the time, with all classes. As it happened I was carrying out two other schemes at the same time, both of which involved project-type research methods, neither of which was very successful. A third-year class were attempting a series of group projects on the Industrial Revolution and for the most part were not a bit interested in it. The subject was not very personal to them, there were hardly any local links, and not much to discover which was not known and easily avail-able. This produced the usual crop of sheaves of writing copied straight from textbooks, and little shared experience between the groups. Perhaps I did not disguise the fact that I found the list of inventions and advances a little boring too, but these pitfalls of projects are difficult to avoid.

The second scheme was also with a second-year class, and also on the Armada. This set was the other side of the coin from the one I have been describing so far: a top set, bright as buttons, but with only five boys, and work always very carefully and meticulously done. Using much the same resources I wanted to try something more ambitious, encouraged by the success of my Armada project the lower set. I split them into groups and gave each group a topic with to research, centred on the events of 1588; each group was to produce one piece of visual material at least, which I would get photographed on to a slide, and a commentary on it which would be tape-recorded. The result would, therefore, be an illustrated talk prepared by the class. This is an idea that I shall try again some-time, but it just did not get off the ground with the group I chose. For one thing, I only saw them three times a fortnight, so enthu-siasm flagged between lessons; for another, I had pushed them into their topics, and they consequently lacked any real enquiring attitude. Most of the girls were reluctant to put their voices on tape, and the work was usually very stilted in the 'potted biography' style: 'Sir Francis Drake was born in 1545 and first went to sea in . . . etc.' Some of the maps and pictures of ships were beautifully drawn, but I felt that throughout the work I had been forcing the pace, without their really being interested, so the scheme was quietly allowed to fade out. I hope to try it again, when it is truly a class effort, not my effort carried out by the class.

Interest still remained in the original set, however, and to bring the work of all the groups together in some kind of shared experi-ence, which I think is necessary at the end of a project, each person 'became' one of the people involved in the Armada story. I 'inter-viewed' them to make a thirty-minute 'radio programme' of the event as seen through the eyes of the participants. Some wrote their contributions out, others spoke 'off the cuff':

Sir Alec: Quickly, Sir Kevin, the Armada is on its way.

Sir Kevin: No hurry, Sir Alec, we will wait until the tide is right and by then they will be past us, so we will have the wind behind us.

Sir Alec: I say we try to get out in front of them to stop them going up the Channel.

Sir Kevin: If this westerly wind holds, we would be defeated; anyway, I want to finish my game of bowls.

Sir Alec: I disagree completely. If the Spaniards decide to invade they could choose any port on the south coast of England and we could not stop them.

Sir Kevin: I don't care what you say, we go out after the Armada passes and gain the wind. It is a chance we will have to take.

Sir Alec: All right, I give in, but if we lose we will all blame you.

All this was accompanied with a great deal of gesticulating and argument over a map Gary had drawn. Christine would not record her voice but wrote a diary of an English captain which one of the boys read, part of which ran:

7th day at sea. Ammunition running low and food supplies scarce. Gave my sister-ship 'Undine' as a fire-ship to help break up this Spanish line. We shall starve before we defeat them at this rate.

8th day at sea. You never did see such a sight as the Spanish ships running away from the fire-ships at top speed.

9th day at sea: Fought for three hours near Gravelines. Sank a large Spanish galleon, the 'San Rachele' for the loss of two killed and ten wounded on my ship when our mizzen mast fell. . . .

13th day at sea: Gave up the chase. Spaniards still flying north in strong wind. Went into Tynemouth to see to our wounded and collect fresh water. Praise be to God for His good fortune and helpful winds.

One of the perpetually high-spirited boys decided to be a Spanish cabin-boy:

Hello there. I am a cabin-boy on the galleon 'San Martin'. I have to work very hard to keep our position in the crescent formation our commander has lined up. Our captain is very strict. He has already given me ten lashes with the whip for spilling his soup. Now the English are sending their secret weapon, burning ships which will explode. Si, si, captain; he has told me to cut the anchor-rope to get away. Now we are sailing north fast. I hope we get home.

Transcripts cannot really capture the dramatic quality and historical interest of some of the work. Here is Peter's description of his watch by the beacon:

I am waiting until I see the Armada come. If it does come I have to light the beacon and all the beacons light up all the way to London. We don't know when they will come, so I've just got to wait and watch. It is getting dark now. Look at those lamps! Quick, pass the torch! There, that's caught light now. Look at the next beacon, they've seen our light.

Peter was a very mild and placid boy, who knew the beacon well, and I am sure that to him the event really did take place on the cliff above the sea among the bracken. His accent was quite broad too, as were most of the others, which gave a certain amount of dramatic and historical validity to the work. It seems to me very

satisfactory that children like Alec and Peter, who have great difficulty writing, should get used to tape-recorders as a means of
expression. We had only a rather large one, but a portable
cassette-type, with regular use, could greatly increase the contribution such children can make. Further, it would give them a
medium in which they are not doomed to failure, but can achieve
some self-respect through their work.

The fact that this was a bottom set did not make for easy teaching, and even at this early stage there was some of the resentment
and bitterness towards school and teachers which makes fourth-
year bottom streams so difficult to cope with. Lumped together in
the one class were children with all sorts of problems, from technical ones of reading and writing to various degrees of maladjust-
ment, and I found that a double lesson with them left me tired and
irritable, particularly towards the end of term. Each child needs a
great deal of personal attention and could not get much assistance
from his classmates as they were all pretty much the same in ability.
In theory, setting is intended to allow the most able children to be
pushed on, the less able to be treated as a whole; in practice the
children lose out at both levels in the vital matter of individual
attention, as teachers can conveniently think of them as all the
same. Some of these effects of setting on both groups could be
avoided by unstreaming them. Fortunately I was able to make some
comparisons here as I also took three third-year classes, each com-
prising the whole range of ability, and although I do not feel I
have got very near to mastering the problem of teaching mixed
ability groups, it was a very interesting experience.

Perhaps the most obvious consequence of unstreaming a class is
that the teacher is immediately faced with the fact that the amount
of time he can spend talking to the whole class is cut right down.
In a true, i.e. uncreamed, Comprehensive School, a mixed-ability
class will contain pupils who will go on to further education, those
who will leave school as early as they can, and all the grades in
between. I found that children in their third year were in many
ways at the most volatile stage in their Secondary School career:
no longer overawed by teachers, yet not quite ready to discipline
themselves to any real extent. Clearly this depends largely on the
schools and their teaching policy from infant schools onwards, but
in the circumstances in which I found myself, it was soon made all
too obvious to me when a child had lost interest in what was going
on. This was, therefore, far more likely to happen in talking to a
mixed-ability class where it was virtually impossible to avoid being
boring to the above-average children, or unintelligible to the

F

below-average children, or both. Therefore, for most of the time the children will be working on their own, or in groups, and the occasions when they are all involved in a class lesson will be strictly limited. The best occasions for these sessions are probably as 'lead' lessons containing material of general interest which should be as interesting as possible to stimulate further investigation at all sorts of levels.

Apart from these considerations, I much prefer getting away from my desk at the front and talking to individuals and groups anyway. After some inept floundering at the beginning of the year the first piece of work we embarked on, that was anything like it should have been, was on medieval towns. As a start, I had shown a film-strip on medieval towns, which was not particularly good, in fact, and then, with a number of pictures, we had talked about a medieval town near by which had a considerable medieval quarter still intact. Then I gave out work-sheets which started with some very simple and specific tasks arising out of the film-strip and our discussion: write a list of some of the shops from the film, draw a plan of one of the merchants' houses, for example. After that came more general topics for enquiry, together with book lists, including in most cases, page references. At the end there were a number of suggestions for imaginative work, arising out of the particular line of enquiry that the pupil had followed up. I walked around from group to group giving help and advice when I could, but trying to avoid supplying ready-made answers.

In one particular class these were some of the things that happened: Lynne and Heather, two extremely intelligent girls, were soon embarked on following up, in pictures and words, the trades of the town and how the craftsmen worked. Usually their work is exquisitely illustrated and written, sometimes at the expense of thoroughness, and they needed to be egged on to follow things through and stretch themselves. Later they produced reference books from home, and generally worked well. Another group of girls was dissuaded from doing clothes and fashion in medieval England, not because it was not a worthwhile topic, but because it is so often a soft option for girls, and there is more to history than fashion. One girl last year used the same material for a project on fashion in history, English and needlework lessons; I suppose she deserves credit for revealing how absurd the subject divisions are, but it did mean that she avoided doing any original work for weeks. Other children worked at roads and transport, castles, fairs and town government. I was able to produce some facsimiles of early charters and documents for the city near by, which provided a good deal of interest in this last case. The non-readers, who had been such a problem in the bottom second-year set because there were so many of them and whose presence so restricted the material I could use, were, in this mixed-ability group, restricted to two. One worked with his friends, who helped him along but made sure he did his fair share, but the other, named Eddie, was rather an isolate, and usually too shy or self-absorbed to ask for help. He tried hard, but was of well below average intelligence, and needed a great deal of attention. He decided that he liked the look of medieval houses and I suggested that he looked for as many different designs, using as many different materials, as he could find. This took him way outside the medieval period, but I felt that this did not matter very much. He became absorbed in this, and spent ages thumbing through books; while this may not be a bad thing for a child to whom books are perhaps suspect and alien, his production of written work was negligible. However, I have no doubt that in a streamed situation it would have been even more negligible, as he became lost among his more noisily demanding classmates. At least in this mixed-ability situation he was a problem I could spend time on without interference.

An ideal follow-up to this piece of work on the town would have been some practical work of some kind: model-making, perhaps a diorama of a town, to which everyone could contribute comething, and academic classifications would become largely irrelevant. However, I saw the class for only two single lessons a week, and the room was totally unsuitable for this kind of activity anyway. Of course these are lame excuses and there are ways round them: co-operating with the Art and Craft Department, changing rooms or running lunch-time sessions. Perhaps it is a measure of the stresses of first-year teaching that the lame excuses seem overwhelming at the time.

However, I think it is worth pointing out that teaching a mixed-ability class effectively involves far more than the changes in teaching attitude that I have described. Merely to put thirty children of varying ability in the same room as a teacher, for two lessons a week called history, falls far short of the ideal. For many of the children, the unstreamed group was unusual for them, as they were streamed for Maths, English, Sciences and Languages and they lacked experience in this type of learning. Broad, open-ended questions were not popular, and answers were too often just copied from large chunks of the textbook. Enquiry-type learning has to be built up to, and the children gradually familiarised with its methods over a sustained period. I also allowed them to work in their normal friendship groups, which usually meant that each child was with someone of roughly the same ability. I would have liked to establish 'family groups' on primary school lines with four or five children of different abilities helping each other, but the children resented leaving friends, and two periods per week were hardly going to break the pattern of the other thirty-three. With mixed-ability classes a statement is not only being made about children, but about learning, which is not restrained by subject boundaries and bell-times, by tightly organised syllabuses and meagre time allowances. The school is in a somewhat transitional stage at the moment and will no doubt be coming to terms with the wider implications of unstreaming in due course, but this year with mixed-ability classes has been a little frustrating as a result.

The frustrations have, however, been relieved by one or two moderately successful approaches which developed over the course of the year. The first involved the preparation of an archive kit on the local Poor Law and its workings. I had prepared a small kit of about twenty documents during my year at the University of Sussex, under the guidance of Colin Brent; the subject, the rise and fall of the Cinque Port of Winchelsea, had been of great interest to me and I learned a great deal from its preparation, but many of the more interesting documents were medieval or sixteenth century, with the result that it was only useful in school at sixth-form level. On the whole, documents are far more plentiful, more varied, and more legible after 1800, which is important from a teaching point of view. This leaves plenty of subjects open for preparing kits, but is possibly the one great limiting factor. I worked with a colleague this time, and we chose the Poor Law as a well-documented topic, and a way of beginning to use archives in this school. Immediately we were faced with the choice of either trying to find fifty or sixty usable extracts, so that each child had at least two different ones to work from on his own, or a smaller number duplicated, so that each child had his own set, rather like the University of Sheffield kits. The former is the ideal, as the sets can be passed round and each child has the opportunity of completing several small pieces of research, but the latter was chosen for reasons of time, both teaching time, during which they would be used, and our time in preparing the kit. We can always add to the kit in future years. Fifteen documents was our eventual total, varying from letters, through plans, posters, newspaper articles and official letters, to *Oliver Twist*. The 'Hawthorne Effect' (that any new scheme succeeds just because it is new and enthusiastically backed) was very powerful here, as I got a great kick out of handling original documents in a way that I had never done for a degree. Our local record office was very helpful and although we did not find events on the scale of the famous Andover Workhouse Scandal, the documents did contain a wealth of personalities, details and flavour of the times, that any other treatment of the topic could not possibly have achieved. We had the *Reading Mercury* article, describing the setting up of the Speenhamland System, various settlement certificates, including names that I knew were local, and vestry records of outdoor relief. There were a whole series of documents on the setting up of the workhouse and its rules and regulations, including posters for the sale of village almshouses within the Union, hints of a well-concealed outbreak of disease in the workhouse in the 1860's, and the apprenticeship regulations, culminating in *Oliver Twist*. One or two documents were purely illustrative, but there were quite definite pieces of information to be gained from most of them, and by putting them together, perhaps with additional information from us, series of deductions could be made.

In using these documents in the classroom, I put them together in twos or threes, centred on one topic. Many of the children found the unusual handwriting and language rather intimidating at first, so were led into the documents by means of very simple questions. I hope that as this approach increases, documents will be as familiar as textbooks, and once the realisation had come that the documents were just sources of information—more particularly, *the* sources of information—then the class worked well at the more general questions they were set. Given that they were a mixed-ability class, I altered the questions according to the children, although not, I admit, always very successfully. Lynne and Heather wrote diaries of paupers before and after the 1834 Poor Law. Others produced some very fine sketches of the workhouse, taken from nineteenth-century prints. Eddie found an account of an apprentice boy who hated his master and ran away, from the Vestry Minute Book of his village. He wrote a story about him which was wildly inaccurate in details, but we spent what I think was a very important ten minutes going over the story and checking it where we had the documents. The importance of evidence was a valuable lesson for most of the class, as I insisted on an authority for every statement made. Two boys wanted to write an account of the Board of Guardians meeting where the medical report on the outbreak of measles was discussed; this led them to medical dictionaries, books on costume, and to the Quennells' excellent *History of Everyday Things*, to find out details. Part of their dialogue ran:

Earl of Wessex: Well, gentlemen, I think the doctors have exaggerated the problem. After all these poor people don't eat well in their own homes.

Mr. Dunhill: I agree your Lordship. Our diet has been approved at Mr. Chadwick himself. The gruel is excellent and the size of helpings is very generous.

Mr. Cosworth (quietly fingering his stock): I have heard that some of the poor men have fainted while doing their three and a half hours at the treadmill. Perhaps they are weak.

Earl of Wessex: Stop fidgeting and talking rubbish, Cosworth. The men were probably trying to get out of working. We were not appointed Her Majesty's Guardians of a holiday hotel, you know.

I don't usually like asking for poems from children as I myself would resent having to write poetry to order, so always give an alternative; however, Heather produced a 'Lament for Mabel Baxter':

> Mabel Baxter, old, a widow
> Eyes grown dim and head hung low,
> Lost her job; she could not manage,
> Rheumatism made her slow.
>
> Though she'd lived for sixty years,
> In the village beside the bay
> Down to the workhouse ward they sent her
> In the city, miles away.
>
> A bowl of soup, and picking oakum
> This was how she spent her day,
> Until disgraced and so neglected
> Mabel Baxter passed away.

Mabel Baxter really was an inmate of the workhouse, and the details are all correct. I also like the poem because it even has a little Victorian sentimentality to it, although I don't think Heather intended this.

As finales to our work on the Poor Law, the school kitchen cooked the meals as prescribed by the Guardians' dietary, and we went to see what was left of the workhouse, and of the medieval houses dealt with earlier in the year. I did feel, on this trip, that in some small way the school had helped the children to understand the places they lived in and the factors which had shaped their lives.

This was particularly important as for many of them these would be the last history lessons they did, because of fourth-year course choices.

Marking work from an unstreamed class presented a problem, as to adopt a common standard would be to reinforce the weak children's sense of failure over and over again. However, the children accepted the solution of each person being marked to his or her own personal standard, far more willingly than I had expected, and with some understanding of what was involved.

Setting work-sheets was a problem too: they did not have the habit or experience of following up their own lines of enquiry, although I suspect that they had done this three years earlier at the primary school. If I set detailed questions, the work-sheets had to be graded according to the ability of the children and this meant knowing them quite well. For a new teacher, seeing some three hundred and fifty children a week, this is a difficult task. Also, if the work-sheets are always graded, the effect is of ten, fifteen, or even thirty different classes in one room, so common group experiences have to be built into the programme. Sometimes this can be done with a homework: after various groups had tackled the quarrel of Becket and Henry II in different ways, I set the task of writing a newspaper (a useful anachronism) for December 29th 1170. All the class could display the knowledge they had picked up, and add extra touches of their own, depending on what they had done, and the standard I expected from them. In Lynne's paper, for example, amongst several articles, were two advertisements: 'Have you taken your tithe to the tithe-barn yet? If you haven't, take it in a strong sack—a Worzel Sack. Only $\frac{1}{2}$d each'. and 'Have your trial the loyal way, come to the King's Court right away'. Marking this kind of exercise does require a careful watch on everyone's standards, as it could be easy for a child to get away with second-best when there is no common standard expected from the set. With this in mind, however, I have seen no evidence that brighter children lose out in a mixed-ability class, as its opponents fear; in fact, rather to the contrary, my experience is that they gain in many ways from working on their own and setting their own standards. Certainly, socially, the results are much happier.

With work-sheets fluttering and children working, I would have been tempted to ignore one of John Townsend's main points of the previous year: the need for variety of approach. Work-sheets are *a* learning method, but not *the* learning method. Fortunately children are not slow to tell you when they are bored, and took the wind out of my sails more than once with 'Not rotten old work-sheets again, sir', as I appeared with another carefully prepared bundle. Having admitted to not exploring modelling as an alternative activity, I can say that I have been able to do a good deal of drama this year, which, like modelling, has the added great advantage of rendering academic distinctions between the children almost entirely irrelevant.

Drama is well established at school, and I took two lessons a week of drama myself. This has great advantages as it means that the children are quite prepared to experiment and improvise, and need much less guidance. I don't like the idea of prepared scripts learned beforehand, with carefully rehearsed movements and meticulous costumes; even if the script is written by the children it can be drudgery for them, and still leaves far too much of the initiative and control in the hands of the teacher. In experienced hands the resulting play can look most effective, but it is little more than a teacher's puppetry, without much educational value. Ideally, just as every history-teaching room should have a sink and modelling tables to hand, so it should also have easy access to a convenient and well-equipped hall or drama laboratory. In fact, by thinking ahead and persuading the kitchen staff to alter their routine, we sometimes managed to borrow the dining-hall for a lesson.

In the case of the Becket story, upon which we built an improvised play, I split the class into five or six groups, and the only people I actually cast were Becket and Henry. We had talked about the issues involved in a previous lesson, and I had read to them the description of Becket's death from the medieval chronicle. Each group were responsible for part of the story, from the group of girls who set the scene in Canterbury market-place, to the murder and Henry's penance. As the children were experienced in this sort of work, I was able to leave a great deal of the details to them and walked between the groups checking what was happening, and discussing details. The only people I worked closely with were the four knights, Becket and two monks, for the climax, but even here they had more ideas than I did about how to 'die' well, and how to strike with a sword, and built up a very menacing atmosphere. The action flowed all over the hall, with different areas for different places, and after some time I let them use the bits and pieces in the costume box: pieces of costumes, materials, belts, hoods, a tattered crown, not proper costumes but enough to suggest character and give their imaginations more to work on.

Each group ran through several ideas, and we discussed what was to be the final version. The only words committed to paper were one or two key sentences which were cues to important changes in the action. In the next lesson, we had brief rehearsals to get back into the parts, then ran the whole piece through. The first episode was in Canterbury market-place, where the women very realistically set up stalls, haggled (and incidentally used a great deal of knowledge from previous lessons), and then cheered and discussed Henry and Becket as they rode through the town. We then had a trial of a criminous clerk, escaping the leering jailer by stumbling through a reading from a hymn-book, and a very noisy and drunken banquet scene at Henry's court. Henry, accompanied by a lady who, I gathered, was certainly not his wife, cursed Becket, and the knights galloped off round the hall. The mood changed to the calm of the cathedral, the knights entered, taunted and stalked Becket, and then savagely cut him down. Henry's penance provided a kind of epilogue. Apart from the dramatic value of this work, I am sure it was historically valuable too. At every stage, one of the aims of a history teacher must be to involve the intellect and feelings of the pupil, and not allow his lessons to become merely passive experiences for the children; in drama, even if only for five minutes during an otherwise ordinary lesson, the pupil is involved in experiencing a historical situation as nearly as he possibly can. This one that I have described raised all sorts of questions: what did they eat? what did they wear? what happened to the knights? what was Henry like? what was Becket like? In answering these questions the pupils learned from each other to apply intelligence and imagination in finding solutions that they felt were right.

The two classes I have described so far, have both been involved in work which, while involving training in some aspects of historical skill, is not directly involved with a public examination. For the remainder of a child's school career above this level, however, examinations are usually an overriding element in the work he or she does, and this change is emphasised at the school by a move to another site, five minutes' walk away, formerly occupied by the Grammar School. G.C.E. 'O' level and 'A' level and, to a lesser extent C.S.E., are not very inspiring examinations to work toward, for the most part involving mainly a great deal of memory work and the skill of essay-writing. I was determined not to make this an excuse for giving up experiment and variety in teaching just to concentrate on the body of notes to be covered. A colleague of John Townsend's at Thomas Bennett once remarked that with a bright set he would cover the 'O' level syllabus in the six months before the examination, leaving the previous four terms for work he thought more important and interesting. I wish I had his courage.

However, even while trying to do one's best by the children in terms of their examination results, there are still ways in which the intrinsic interest of the subject can be increased and tasks attempted more worthwhile than mere memory work. For example, the use of documents can add a great deal. Throughout the school I have found that contemporary accounts, often from the *They Saw It Happen* series, give more colour and immediacy to a historical event than any other form of description can. The opportunities for using contemporary accounts were all the greater with my fourth and fifth-year classes, as the syllabus was twentieth-century history. Thus, all sorts of material which was not available for earlier periods could be used: photography and news-reels, for example, as well as a wealth of newspaper, diary, biography and other contemporary accounts, which were both graphic and readable. The Longman's *Modern Times* series and Blond Educational *History Alive*, both include lengthy eye-witness descriptions of key events, and other books consisting solely of documentary evidence, give enormous flexibility to the teaching of this syllabus. I dealt with the rise of Nazism almost entirely from the book of extracts on the subject in the *Archive Series*, edited by Hill and Fell, which showed up the content and style of Nazi writing and speeches far more effectively than I could have done.

Apart from being an all-important stimulus of interest, the use of documents can provide interesting and worthwhile tasks for the children. A comparison, for example, of the report from the *Daily Telegraph*, *The Times* and the *Daily Worker* of Mussolini's march on Rome in 1922 gives us not only details of the event, and a sidelight on the attitude to it of people in England, but also an important exercise in detecting bias in what appears at first sight to be straightforward reporting. For the sixth form, I compiled work from two different historians on the same events, to the same sort of effect. I used the same theme later with the fourth year after we had dealt with the death of Trotsky, and set the homework of writing two obituaries, one from *Pravda*, the other from an English newspaper. The class did not find this easy and only those with more maturity of judgement really answered the problem in the way I had hoped; but if examinations have to sort people out, this seems one more appropriate way of doing it.

Under the loose category of documents can come all sorts of material to stimulate interest in a topic and help scotch the image of history teachers as paid story-tellers. On the First World War for example, in addition to official writing, diaries and songs, I used some of Wilfred Owen's poems, and two of Paul Nash's paintings. It was, perhaps, with Paul Nash's 'Menin Road' in mind that a girl included this passage in a long 'letter from the trenches' she wrote as a homework:

> ... We went up front again yesterday, along the Menin Road, the same place as we were last autumn. You can still see our old dugouts, and the bodies of soldiers killed then. The mud is everywhere. Fields, flowers, guns and bodies get buried in it until you can't tell which is which. The remains of supply carts stick up through it like big skeletons. The smell is revolting. How I wish it was all over and I could come back to you and the children. I hope they still remember me. . . .

With such powerful material, the children were almost obliged, not only to receive information, but also to develop opinions. I found that discussion was not something that came easily to them, particularly the kind of abstract discussion that teachers are used to, but given very concrete stimuli, they have something specific to talk about and base their opinions on. For children, discussion is no less a skill to acquire than writing essays, and possibly more use. It also changes the role of the teacher, too, from the provider of information to that of chairman of discussion and poser of problems. Inspired by something similar one of my colleagues at the University of Sussex had done the previous year, I tried out an entertaining example of problem-posing at the end of our study of the First World War: I borrowed an officer's cap and stick from a local army camp, walked in to the lesson and announced that I was Field-Marshal Haig; I talked about 'my' career and tactics during the war, then asked for questions. A lively argument followed, in which nearly everyone had something to say. Obviously this is not something that can be repeated very often, but a good gimmick for occasions.

Many of the things that I have described I would be prepared to admit *were* gimmicks, but once the initial attention and interest of the child is seized, there is an enormous potential motivation to build on. History has a great wealth of fascinating material on which to draw, and once the motivation is there the child can be led to more historical, more educational, goals. Attacks have been made on history recently as too passive a subject for children, lacking in educational value; during the last year, faced with too many lessons to prepare in too short a time, I have resorted far too often to story-telling and mere exposition in order to get by. But nearly always the exercises which I have felt had an educational point to them were valid historically as well, and if that has happened, occasionally, for some classes, I would think the year has had some value.

[1] Sources of documents referred to:

Coulson and Fines for 'Spinners, Society and Industry in 19th century, Factory Reform'. (O.U.P.)

Joseph Sefton, 'Orphan Annie, children in 18th and 19th centuries'. Manchester Manuscripts collected and edited by Manchester branch Historical Association.

Coaches between London and Colchester—'Highways and Byeways of Essex'. (Essex Records Office.)

[2] Sheila Padley, 'A History Project', *Teaching History*, vol. 1, no. 2, pp. 76-82.

[3] Gareth E. Jones, 'Towards a Theory of History Teaching', *History*, 1970, pp. 54-64.

3

BEYOND BEGINNINGS

Colin Brent *Archive Kits*

M Y part in *Beginnings* has been slight. I have discussed with students what seems to me to be the value of the study of local history primarily through the use by the pupil of research units containing a high percentage of materials selected from primary sources. I have argued that the history of the local environment can present the pupil with problems to investigate and interpret which are sophisticated enough to merit a place in the curriculum. I have argued too that this can often best be done by putting before the pupil a wide variety of well prepared and carefully chosen evidence—archival, architectural, archaelogical and topographical, through the use of which he will come to know some of the methods and skills of the historian.

Initial seminar discussion of this argument convinced many students that it was sufficiently plausible to merit testing in practice. For these there followed a visit to the East Sussex County Record Office at Lewes to view the contents of a typical repository. There we tried to discover which classes of archive material, common to most repositories, were of greatest value to teachers selecting materials from which to make research units for local history. Each student chose a theme from the local history of Brighton and East Sussex, constructed a research unit around it and then proceeded to test and evaluate it during school practice. One unit on 'Tudor and Stuart Brighton' was sufficiently successful to merit adoption and circulation by the East Sussex County Council. The whole exercise has highlighted some issues and problems which are worth further discussion.

*　　*　　*

The children in our schools will mature into a society which more and more leaves the individual to make his own political and ethical choices unsupported by detailed and dogmatic codes. Realistic choice will depend in part on a capacity to evaluate evidence and in part on familiarity with a wide range of experience and opinion. The promotion of these capacities should be among the chief aims of those teaching history in our schools. Children should no longer be coerced into committing to memory a chronicle of battle, treaty, king and maypole, forged in the heat of long dead polemic, which is merely 'one damned thing after another'. They should be invited to examine historical themes suited to their developing perceptions and interests. Their own chronology of growth is the best reference point. The study of history is a problem-solving activity, and the teacher's main job should be to formulate realistic research projects and to provide his pupils with evidence relevant to their solution. In this way the child can come to know something of the skills and of the materials needed to make an informed and reasoned choice. He can build up his own models of analysis and construct his own critique of the society within which he must survive. Other subjects which figure in the curriculum are carrying through a 'Nuffield revolution'. The dangers to Western culture posed by political and ethical illiteracy are surely sufficient to require equally drastic change in the aims and methods of history teaching.

At the moment the history of the local environment figures only fitfully and uncertainly in most curricula, yet its inclusion could supply the teacher with many promising themes for research projects and with many fertile sources of evidence. Logistically access to primary source material on local history—documents, maps and prints, is easy and cheap. The best of it is usually available, carefully described and catalogued, in a local record repository, where the staff are equipped and disposed to advise searchers who have familiarised themselves with the sources to some degree. Certain archives particularly fertile in materials for study are official in character and were required by statute. They are to be found in most repositories, wherever the teacher (and the student in training) may happen to teach. Other evidence thrown up by the buildings and landscape of a locality is equally if not more accessible, and it is often being photographed and recorded by local groups of archaeologists, industrial archaeologists, transport historians and preservationists.

Failure to use primary source material which is plentiful, accessible and amenable, robs the study of local history of almost any value. The teacher must rely in part on stringing together those events of 'national significance' which, usually by purest chance, happened to occur in the area—a battle, a treaty, a royal visit, an august resident—a chronicle of capricious and insulated detail. The threadbare distortions of local folklore are desperately pressed into service to provide romanticised generalities about smuggling,

plague, and folk customs which present our ancestors as lunatic—
'Merrie Englande' with a vengeance. When secondary source
material is used it tends to be culled from county and parish
histories compiled in Victorian times and to be administrative,
manorial and ecclesiastical in character. Such antiquarian themes,
even if accurate in their scholarship, can have no meaning for the
average child living in the mid-twentieth century. Much teaching
of local history could never succeed, given the nature of the
materials used.

Many teachers who appreciate the need to acquaint their pupils
with the widest range of evidence nonetheless display a very opti-
mistic view of the unaided research capacity of their pupils. Many
are very prematurely released into libraries or into a wider environment to discover from antiquarian tomes, from bemused librarians
or archivists, or from the more garrulous residents, 'all that they
can' about a person, battle, building or community. Such activity
will almost certainly yield nothing that is worthwhile. Discovery
and interpretation cannot take place in any research situation if the
problems to be investigated are couched in wide and vapid terms
and if nothing is done beforehand to ensure that accessible evidence
exists from which solutions may be worked out.

Initially, of course, the planning of a viable research project into
local history requires the teacher to select a topic which is geared
to the aptitudes and known enthusiasms of his pupils. Secondly he
must ensure that the topic chosen commands sufficient documentary or other evidence to provide adequate materials for its study
and interpretation. Full and prior familiarity with the available
evidence is essential. The teacher must know his sources. Many
potential topics which seem at first sight to be stimulating and
worthwhile have left little or no relevant source material. That
is a discovery which the teacher should make in the course of his
preparations and not the pupils at the close of a sterile research
project.

Once he is satisfied that enough material exists, the teacher then
needs to decide what questions, intellectually stimulating in themselves and requiring the use of analytical judgement and detective
skills for their solution, are most likely to be answered by reference
to that material. This choice of research questions will in turn
decide what aspects of the evidence he will select and present to his
pupils. The planning of research projects involves the teacher in
recognising what aspects of the extant evidence will support the
solution of significant questions. The likely development of the
research will be known and its logistical needs provided for. Pupils

must not be railroaded to discovery; a necessary framework must not become a restricting straitjacket. But if the framework is removed, 'Hark what discord follows'.

The ordering and planning of the materials contained within an archive teaching unit should reflect the teacher's own identification of the research problems which the unit is designed to illuminate. This will often require the division of the unit into half a dozen or more clusters of evidence, each illustrating a single research problem. The problems to be solved may be loosely sequential and require the child or the group to work through the unit in a certain order, or they may each contribute independently to the building of a total picture, which will allow each unit to be worked on simultaneously by individuals or groups. Units will remain mere medlies of isolated facts unless the selection and arrangement of items has been determined by a grasp of their research potential as related items.

A final problem for the teacher may be the degree to which the source material chosen for his research unit needs to be altered in format. It seems important that facsimile copies of original documents should be included in most units if possible. Their antique appearance may cause a measure of curiosity and excitement which is valuable, although usually ephemeral. Their presence does however impress on the researcher that knowledge of the past is based on source materials which need interpretation in a variety of ways. They do not come printed in textbooks or typed in folders. In practice almost all facsimiles of archival material earlier in date than the later eighteenth century will need to be accompanied in the unit by a transcription and, if in Latin, by a translation, although the reforming zeal of the Commonwealth period instituted for a decade the use of English in legal documents. Paraphrase may avoid the tedium of legal common form and the obscurity of legal idiom. There is nothing sacred about archival format; it should be ruthlessly transformed, if necessary, to make the evidence which it contains manageable for the researcher. Authenticity must be balanced against ease of interpretation.

The format of some of the most valuable source material for the nineteenth century poses other problems. The schedules, reports and completed questionnaires which snowball as the century progresses are cumbrous to handle and immense in the range of detail which they contain. Unless the teacher selects his relevant material and includes it in his unit in tabulated or statistical form, these sources will remain charnels of inert information. If pre-digested and packaged, the evidence contained in enumerators' books and in tithe map schedules can in themselves underpin entire research projects.

Some care should be taken to diversify the material by the inclusion of pictorial material—plans, maps, prints and photographs, if they are genuinely and relevantly informative. Much such material is included in most commercially prepared units and it is usually highly glossed, colourful and excellently reproduced. Yet often, in spite of its sophistication, such material cannot be integrated into a scheme of research because it contains no evidence useful for the solution of problems. It hangs, therefore, unused and disregarded on the classroom wall—sugar to coat a bitter pill of fact.

*   *   *

Certain categories of document which are especially valuable sources of evidence for teachers planning research units in local history are common to almost all county record offices. Those dating from the 1830's onwards are increasingly numerous and amenable. These committee minutes, annual reports and audits, decennial censuses and ordnance surveys, reflect in part a reformed administration of local government which depended on elected committees responsible to the ratepayers and to inspectors from the central government and in part a need for detailed and systematically collected data on which to base an increasing government intervention into social and economic life. Such materials offer ample evidence to support research projects into the social structure and the social philosophy of the Victorian period through a study of institutions or of rural and urban communities. Besides their intrinsic historical value, such researches allow useful comparative studies of similar institutions and communities at the present day, thereby highlighting many of the significant social changes which have taken place over the last hundred years or so.

The records of many Victorian institutions survive—workhouses, prisons, hospitals and asylums, from which a picture may be built up of their design and construction, their financing and management, their staffing and establishment, the routine which was required of their inmates and the philosophy of man and of society which underlay that routine. Research into such institutions should culminate in an appreciation of the theories about mental health, about crime and punishment and about poverty and welfare provision which they embody in their architecture, their equipment and their regulations. The provision from 1870 of rate-supported education in publicly controlled elementary schools

G

created more documentation of which the school log-book is perhaps the most useful for unit construction. From it can often be built up a detailed picture of life in the Victorian classroom—the accommodation and apparatus, the time-table and discipline, the treats and holidays, the attendance and epidemics, and above all, the curriculum and the methods by which it was taught. From such material something may be deduced about contemporary views on learning, on childhood and on the role of education, and their contrast with those held today, if any.

Source materials for the study of both rural and urban parishes are especially informative for the 1840's, 1850's and 1860's. Particularly important are the survival in the Public Record Office in London of the enumerators' books made for the decennial censuses of 1841, 1851 and 1861. These books contain the household questionnaires from which the published census material was abstracted. They give the location of each household and the age, the sex, the relationship to the head of the household, and the status or occupation of each member of the household. In 1851 and 1861 the parish of birth is also given. Most record offices now have microfilms of the 1861 census; the others may be freely consulted in London. Population figures published in each decennial census between 1801 and 1911 allow the fuller picture available for these three decades to be set in a longer perspective of population change. Parish registers may provide further information on individuals.

Such detailed evidence allows the selection of material which can support a variety of research questions. Was the Victorian household larger than the modern one on average? Were there normally three generations living under one roof with an assortment of cousins in the garrets and outhouses? How widespread was the employment of servants? What was the average age of the population and what was its age structure? In what ways did people earn their living? How many householders were paupers? What forms of employment common then are unknown today? How true is the popular belief that people during this period tended to live and to die in the parish in which they were born? What occupation groups, if any, seem to have been the most mobile? Again a parallel and comparative study of the same community at the present time would establish the degree of continuity and isolate areas of change requiring explanation. These decades are sufficiently close to us culturally to be comprehensible and yet sufficiently remote to show interesting divergencies from our own.

Maps are likely to be valuable aids to research since the data which they contain has already been subjected to selection and arrangement. It has been predigested. Maps proliferated in the nineteenth century to satisfy the contemporary thirst for information. Privately published county and borough maps with a large and accurate scale appear in the later eighteenth century. The 1″ Ordnance Survey begun during the Napoleonic wars was supplemented by a 6″ Survey from 1840 and a 25‴ Survey from 1853. Some towns were mapped on a 10·56 ft. to a mile scale in the 1870's, a scale sufficiently large to show garden paths, post-boxes and the layout of rooms in larger buildings. The national surveys were each periodically revised. But most informative of all is the tithe map on a 25″ scale produced in the 1840's for the majority of parishes. On it is represented every enclosure of land, every field, wood, garden, pond, every building and larger outhouse, every road, stream and waterway and many footpaths. An accompanying schedule lists the name, or description, the acreage, the land use, the owner and the occupier of each numbered unit on the map. The tithe map is probably the most valuable quarry of evidence, for the planning of research into local history, available to the teacher.

From this map material further aspects may be studied of the character of rural and urban parishes in the earlier Victorian period. In rural parishes lines of enquiry which would be supported by such evidence include the nucleated or dispersed pattern of settlement, the character of the agriculture and the balance between arable, pastural and woodland farming, the influence on settlement, communications and farming of the local geology, relief and water supply, the nature of the field systems, the size and number of the home farms, the tenant farms and the small-holdings, the meaning of field and place names, and the extent of common land. The necessary inclusion in such a unit of map material illustrating local geology, drainage and relief will oblige the researcher to break through the time-honoured barriers which hem in the province of history; much of his work will be in the uneasy border zone of historical geography.

The ownership of land in the Victorian countryside was the main source of economic power, social prestige and political influence. Therefore the extent to which land ownership in a rural parish was concentrated in the hands of a single family or of a few substantial residents or scattered among small-holders profoundly affected the character of the parish. The presence of a substantial body of small-holders might give it a Liberal and a Nonconformist tinge; domination by a powerful landowner might reduce it to a Tory-Anglican subservience. What the balance was may be found from study of the tithe map evidence and its impact on politics and religion may sometimes be investigated by examination of poll books and contemporary newspaper reports and, less hopefully, of church and chapel records.

But the balance may often be reconstructed in part from a study of the architecture and the landscape of a parish. The presence of a great house, a park, a model village or model farmsteads and cottages, a family pew and a family vault in the church, and a coat of arms on the sign board of the public house, may each testify to a landowning family's local power. Such a family may have rebuilt the church, the almshouses and the school which may display its escutcheon carved above the date of the rebuilding—vivid evidence also of the influence exerted by paternalism over education and welfare provision. By contrast a village centre full of houses of comfortable proportions but idiosyncratic design and boasting a chapel and a co-operative store, may corroborate what the documents reveal, the presence of entrenched small-holders and independent craftsmen. The inclusion in a unit of photographic evidence illustrating these features of landscape and architecture represents for me a correct use of pictorial material to reinforce a theme rather than to decorate it for light relief.

Study of the buildings of a parish may reinforce the evidence for other aspects of its history. Many village homes exhibit architectural features which give a clue to the commercial enterprises carried on within them or within their outhouses—a miller's loft, a wheelwright's yard, a blacksmith's forge from which a garage has evolved, the large cellars and spreading road frontage of a former public house. The building materials used in the parish will show how close was the dependence on local sources of flint, clay or stone until the coming of cheap railway transport. Only the church and the great house built to the glory of God and the landed classes could command expensive materials brought from outside the locality. This balance has been reversed since the coming of the railway so that now only prestige buildings incorporate local materials. The chronology of this change can often be worked out from the surviving architectural evidence.

Research into the urban development of the nineteenth century usually centres around the identification and correlation of changes in employment, transport and population. The enumerators' books and the decennial census provide a wealth of evidence for the character of employment and the growth of population. The periodic revision of ordnance survey maps and the profusion of other map material allows the researcher to identify the streets of new housing needed to accommodate a growing population and to establish by further reference to the enumerators' books and to directories the predominant employment of their new householders. The names of the streets and of the houses and terraces often reflect the heroes or the aspirations of the period which built them. The build-up of amenities to serve the 'Newtowns'—parish churches, dissenting chapels, elementary schools, dispensaries and tramways, may also be traced from map material, and from newspaper reports, in which their architectural decency, their sensible design and their certain contribution to the inevitable progress of the Empire and the Nation were proclaimed. Many such houses and buildings survive with their date plaques, their foundation stones and their period styles to add visual material to the range of evidence.

Transport developments have normally played a dynamic part in the diversification of urban employment and the growth (or decay) of urban populations. From the early eighteenth century an Act of Parliament was needed before any innovation in transport facilities could be made. The Act set out the purpose and location of the proposed turnpike road, inland navigation, railway or harbour work, the names of the trustees, the legitimate scale of tolls and charges which might be levied. The Act also required a detailed plan of the proposed new line of communication and the property through which it must pass, to be deposited with the clerk of the peace in the county concerned. Copies of relevant Acts of Parliament authorising transport changes and of deposited plans are normally to be found in the local record office concerned. From such material the development of communications in any locality can be firmly established and linked with economic and population growth, and a basis laid for further research into the identity and business connections of the promoters, the cost of carriage and the type of traffic envisaged. Roads, canals and railways are among the most indestructible of landscape features and their remains are enlisting fanatical interest and study from industrial archaeologists and transport historians. Visual material is consequently often very easy to obtain. The topic is perhaps the most rapid growth point in local history at the present time.

'Only connect' is a fashionable moral aphorism, but it might also with profit be a guiding principle for those preparing research units into local history. The formulation of accurate information from source materials is a useful and necessary preliminary stage in research, but all too often it remains the final achievement. The abundant research materials extant from the nineteenth century allow many aspects of a topic or theme to be examined in detail and their format established. But into the unit should be built a secondary stage of research in which these aspects are compared, correlated and connected and some possible causal links uncovered. The relationship between penal methods and penal theory, between the contents of a curriculum and a current theory of education, between employment and mobility, between a pub sign, a family pew and land ownership, between transport, employment and population growth—these relationships once connected become models of analysis which will contribute to an ever-growing sophistication of interpretation. The making of connections between data should be the final objective of research units.

Documentary sources for the study of local history prior to the eighteenth century present problems for those preparing research units. Extant archives in local record offices from the medieval period are almost entirely of legal origin written in Latin in a difficult script and in a formal style using obscure terminology. Worse still their subject matter is normally confined to property settlements, estate and household accounts and the transaction of manorial business. The Tudors created a strong central and local administration which has left, from the Elizabethan period onwards, a wide range of extant official records, often in English, although usually written in an abominable script. These cover the administration of the parish—the registration of baptisms, marriages and burials, the expenditure and duties of the church-wardens, the overseers of the poor and the overseers of the highways—of the corporate boroughs—the election of the mayor, the aldermen and freeman and often the Members of Parliament, the levying of rates, the making of by-laws governing the market, the harbour, plague, sanitation and defence—and of the county—the work of the justices at quarter-sessions in punishing crime and vagrancy, maintaining roads and bridges, fixing wages and prices, guarding against plague and famine and inquiring into pockets of poverty or unrest. The most complete and informative of such records have often been printed by local archaeological or historical societies.

Except for the land-tax returns which often begin in 1692 and give an annual list of the owners and often the occupiers of landed property in a parish, and for Acts of Parliament and accompanying documentation authorising the enclosure of open fields and common land, no new official records valuable to the local historian appear after the great Tudor reorganisation of England until the Whig-Utilitarian revolutions of the early nineteenth century. Moreover, although the scripts improve and the language after

1731 is invariably English, the documents themselves become increasingly formal, thin and uninformative, with the valuable exception of inventories. By contrast a growing number of business and personal papers survive although inevitably from the wealthier classes. Little remains which can easily and comprehensively illustrate local economic, social and population change except generalisations made by the new breed of topographers—Celia Fiennes, Daniel Defoe, Arthur Young and William Cobbett. Even anecdotal information about the lower classes, or wage-earners, craftsmen and small-holders is rare. Such people remain virtually anonymous until the compilation of the enumerators' books.

The uneven survival and varying detail of such archive material makes generalisation on its research potential difficult. However, for the eighteenth century three related themes seem promising— the enclosure of open fields, the organisation of farming and the culture of the great country estate.

The open-field system is often presented in textbooks, abstracted from any earthly context, as a universal feature of medieval farming developed to ensure equality of economic opportunity and abolished on the morrow of Bosworth Field. The national course of parliamentary enclosure in the eighteenth century is more sophisticatedly treated to meet standard 'O' level requirements. A study of local open fields and enclosure should include the factors of geology and relief which limited the development of open-field agriculture to certain areas or determined the internal layout of a parish's open fields. Manorial courts' records normally contain periodic statements of the common farming routine required of open-field tenants and owners. The enclosure by parliamentary Act of parochial open fields involved extensive documentation which normally survives, describing and usually mapping the ownership and occupation of the open-field strips and of the new enclosed farms. From the land-tax records the fortunes of the owners under the enclosed system may be traced, and some national generalisations of the consequent extinction of the small-holder tested. An indestructible pattern of ridge and furrow may remain under the local hedgerows imposed upon it. A local network of streets may follow ancient divisions between fields and furlongs as at Brighton. If relevant inventories survive, some idea may be gained of the crop rotations used, the livestock kept and the level of household comfort achieved.

The legal and personal papers accumulated by landed families have often been deposited in local record offices. These sources may give an intimate picture of that élitist culture based on the possession of a great country estate which reached a splendid summit of influence in the eighteenth century. Estate maps, deeds and leases record the build-up and extent of the estate, account books list the rents and other revenues and the expenditure on wages, repairs and hospitality, inventories catalogue the furniture, pictures and sculpture, diaries chronicle the social round, architect's and surveyor's plans illustrate the rebuilding of the mansion and the remodelling of the park. The mansion and park often survive more or less battered and eager to welcome parties of researchers at reduced rates. The sophistication of this culture patronised by the English aristocracy in the eighteenth century was unequalled in contemporary Europe, yet it remained focused on the country house and was financed in part from the estate which surrounded it. The elements which composed such a harmonious balance are promising objects of research.

Elizabethan 'town life' figures in most textbooks rather gamely as a riotous amalgam of wassail, stocks, wenches and half-timbering —to be drawn, coloured in and 'imaginatively' regurgitated for homework. Yet sufficient archival and topographical evidence often survives to allow detailed investigation of the realities of urban history in the Elizabethan and early Stuart period. Two towns in East Sussex, Rye and Brighton, may be cited to demonstrate this.

The extensive corporation records of Rye have been catalogued by the East Sussex Record Office and long extracts have been published by the Historical Manuscripts Commission. The Sussex Record Society has printed for the Elizabethan period the Port Books of the town which record the name, port of origin, tonnage and master of each ship using the port, together with details of the cargoes and the merchants shipping them. A fine parish register also exists for the period. Contemporary maps, supplemented by modern aerial photographs and by surviving topographical and architectural evidence, enable the location of the Elizabethan town to be fixed, together with its streets, principal buildings, its walls and gates, its wells and conduits, its harbour and quays. Its substantial population of over 3,000 can be deduced from the annual number of baptisms and marriages recorded in the register. The economy can be reconstructed which gave employment to this population—the transit trade and passenger traffic to and from Dieppe, the coastwise and overseas carriage of iron, timber, glass and leather brought down the River Rother by lighter from a wide hinterland, the import of grain and consumer goods, the operation in local and in North Sea waters of its fishing fleet, the largest in the south-east of England. Fully documented too is the environmental challenge by which the corporation bankrupted the town in a desperate but unsuccessful effort to overcome the silting of its harbour which choked the operation of its fishing fleet and of its merchant marine. The silting brought a series of disasters—a falling off of trade and freight carriage, a withering away of the fishing fleet, a fall in population which left the town impoverished and partly derelict. In this instance the unit can be structured around the results of an unsuccessful response to an environmental challenge.

The research potential of 'Tudor and Stuart Brighton' has been exploited in a kit, largely produced by Pat and now officially adopted by East Sussex Record Office. In it an extremely wide range of documentary evidence (with transcripts) has been arranged to support investigation into seven related aspects of the topic. A commentary serves to remove problems of interpretation, to link the researcher up with a wider national picture, to establish continuity with the present-day character of Brighton and to suggest certain fruitful lines of enquiry. The unit will also serve as a foil for any unit produced on the more well-worn theme of Regency Brighton.

The first section reproduces a Tudor drawing illustrating a French naval attack made on Brighton in 1545. The topography of the town and its neighbourhood is clearly shown—the street plan of the upper and lower town, the small harbour, the parish church set back on a hill, the 'hempshares' in which hemp for nets was grown, and to the west and separated from Brighton by open ground the single street of Hove village. Correlation with a modern street plan of Brighton will reveal to the researcher the identity of the Tudor streets in the upper town, the disappearance of the lower town and of the harbour, the transformation of the 'hempshares' into a pedestrian maze of antique shops and the obliteration of the green belt towards Hove. The second section consists of another reproduction of the drawing and extracts from two chronicle accounts by Hall and by Holinshed describing French naval attacks on Brighton in 1514 and 1545. Besides their narrative interest and their illustration of a variety of shipping—galleons, galleys and fishing boats, these materials contain a valuable problem of interpretation. The drawing is dated 1545 yet it seems to accord with the chronicle account of the 1514 attack. Extracts from manorial and quarter-sessions records and from the State Papers compose a third section on the defence of Brighton—building a blockhouse, maintaining (and neglecting) the artillery within it, reporting and mapping during the Armada crisis the state of coastal defences between Shoreham and Newhaven.

A detailed customal of 1579 describes in exact detail the character of the contemporary fishing industry in the town—the number of men, boats, and nets engaged, the seasons of the fishing year, the types of boats and nets used and the principles governing the distribution of the profits. Extracts from it form the fourth section, together with a facsimile of its cover and of the signatures and marks of the fishermen who attested it. A fifth section draws on quarter-session and State Paper evidence to illustrate the quarrels with neighbouring fishermen, the piracy and unrest in the Channel and the destruction of boats and tackle by erosion of the lower town which combined to impoverish the fishermen and the town in the later seventeenth century. Included also is the caustic comment of Daniel Defoe on the apparent value of the town's assets. An eighteenth-century map of the open fields of Brighton allows a study of the layout of their laines, furlongs and strips and invites a correlation with the street plan of central Brighton. Extracts from the manor court rolls for the Commonwealth period document the institution which recorded all transfers of land, restated the customs regulating open-field agriculture and punished offenders against them.

Finally Pat has succeeded in documenting something of the Puritan-Nonconformist tradition, which was strong in Brighton as in other Sussex seafaring towns, by showing its tenacity in the Carver family. Derek Carver was burnt at Lewes, under Mary, and his declaration of faith at the stake, traditionally ascribed to him, is given. A second Derek Carver is represented by an extract from his will in which he leaves money to support a preaching minister in Brighton on the eve of the Civil War. Finally a facsimile is included of a letter written by George Fox in which he describes a successful plea by Richard Carver, a Quaker of Brighton, to Charles II for the release of imprisoned Friends. Richard Carver had been the mate of the Brighton ship on which the king had escaped to France after his flight from the battle of Worcester.

In general the paucity or thinness of documentary sources for the Stuart, Tudor and medieval periods poses problems for those planning research units. These may be partly overcome by the choice of topics which can with profit be studied at a county or regional level rather than at a parochial level. This will enable the use of whatever relevant documentation is extant. The planning of such units can be further eased by an even greater emphasis on surviving architectural and topographical evidence, and perhaps on occasion by a complete reliance upon it. Units of this character constructed for use in East Sussex might include studies of the Wealden iron industry, of the settlement and clearance of the county and of the emergence of Lewes as a regional centre. Such units will depend heavily on the mapping and illustration of data, some of which will need to be tested and reinforced by the provision of fieldwork assignments. Regional research is, of course, valid for any period; indeed much eighteenth and nineteenth century political and economic history has been rewritten in the light of it. However, for an earlier period the region is often the only viable unit of study.

A study of the Wealden iron industry during the late Tudor and early Stuart periods, when it was particularly prosperous, might well begin by relating the geographical distribution of the known forges and furnaces to the location of the beds supplying the iron ore, the woodland supplying the fuel, the streams providing the power and the rivers providing water-carriage to the ports for the wrought iron and the ordnance and shot. The structure and working of a typical furnace or forge can be appreciated from descriptions and diagrams made in the late seventeenth century and from modern pictorial reconstructions. A variety of evidence may assist in fixing the site of a particular furnace or forge, of which no buildings will remain. Sometimes the site may be mentioned in a document of seventeenth century or later date which also lists the names of adjacent fields or woods. These may often be located on the tithe map. Examination of the same map may reveal names such as 'Forge Wood', 'Furnace Field' and 'Cinder Croft' which commemorate its former presence near by. The site may be exactly pinpointed thereafter by the investigation of nearby streams and the discovery of cinder and slag or of ponds, dams and channels. The evidence will culminate in field-work—a very similar combination of place-name and topographical evidence is used for tracing the line of a Roman road. Finally consideration might be given to traditional explanations given for the decline of the industry.

The gradual settlement and clearance of East Sussex from the arrival of the first Neolithic farmers on the downlands until the vigorous colonisation of the high weald in the thirteenth and the fourteenth centuries, provides another topic which allows the correlation of a variety of evidence on a county-wide scale. The plotting and comparison of distribution maps locating the known Neolithic, Bronze Age, Iron Age and Roman settlements and farms will reveal that they were always concentrated on the chalk downlands.

The other geological zones of the county—the greensand strip at the scarpfoot, the heavy clays of the low weald and the lighter sandier soils of the high wealden uplands, all heavily forested and water-logged in their natural state, these zones were avoided and remained unexploited. Having established the steady preference of the prehistoric farmer for the downland chalk, that preference may in part be explained by reconstructing from excavated evidence something of his farming methods and of the technology at his command.

The Anglo-Saxons largely created in East Sussex two contrasting patterns of villages, farmsteads, fields, roads and place-names each identified with a quite distinct system of farming. These patterns survived basically unaltered into the nineteenth century and they are very clearly represented on large-scale maps of the county made in the eighteenth century. The first is found in the areas of earliest Saxon settlement on the chalk downland around embanked ponds and along the scarpfoot near the spring-line. The place-names often suggest a settlement was made during the migration period and archaeological evidence excavated near by sometimes confirms this. The farming system centred on the cultivation of wheat and barley in open fields on which large flocks of sheep were folded after the harvest. Farmhouses and cottages were concentrated in each parish in a single village; isolated dwellings were few. The roads ran regularly north-south connecting these village centres with their cattle pasture in the weald. The second pattern was created by a later and piecemeal clearance of the forested weald. Large nucleated villages were few. Farms and houses were isolated or grouped in hamlets. Farming depended on the breeding of cattle in small, enclosed fields individually owned and rented. Arable farming was unimportant and the open-field system did not exist. Place-names abound in elements, 'hurst', 'field', 'green' and 'end' which suggest forest settlement. The roads still have no logic other that that imposed by the nearest hamlet's need. Each element in these two distinctive patterns has developed in response to environmental factors of geology, drainage and relief. They provide promising materials for the construction of research units into the making of the Sussex landscape.

The emergence of Lewes as a regional centre may be taken as a final topic which can be made the subject of a research unit, even though almost no contemporary documentary evidence survives. Important to the study of any town's development are the factors which have led to the concentration within its walls of a population not primarily engaged in agriculture. The position of Lewes as a 'gap town' situated where the main east-west land route of the county along the scarp of the downs could most easily cross the flood-plain of the River Ouse, the main waterway connecting the weald with the sea, made the town the chief centre of communications for the region and a natural market for the divergent economies of the downland and of the weald, for the sale of barley, wheat, wool, timber, cattle, leather and iron. Its fortification with a castle and with walls recognised its importance as a strategic centre commanding the communications and economy of the region. The security of its defences and the convenience of its position made it a natural centre of regional administration for minting money, assessing taxes and enforcing the laws. Its wealth caused the gravitation to it of cultural and religious institutions, the founding of a rich priory, a friary and of many parish churches.

No archival evidence remains to document the logic of the town's development, but each element in that development can be illustrated from extant topographical and architectural evidence. The major determinants, the scarp route along the downs, the flood-plain of the Ouse, the spur of chalk sloping into it towards the bridge, need no documentation, although they do need mapping. The medieval matrix of Lewes was contained by walls on the eastern tip of the spur and on the west by the castle precinct facing firm and rising ground. The castle, stretches of town wall, the line of the rest, and the regular medieval street plan survive, together with several churches and houses within the walls. The site of the market, the friary, the town gates and several demolished churches within the walls can be pinpointed from place-name evidence. Three medieval suburbs grew up outside the walls, each with its own distinct function and each with an extant medieval parish church. Around the bridge which has been ceaselessly rebuilt but only recently bypassed, an industrial suburb developed which is still marked by a cluster of riverside warehouses, timber yards, a flour mill, a brewery and a foundry. A second, more residential, suburb which still boasts a group of fine Elizabethan and Georgian town houses, grew up on high, healthy and uncramped ground outside the west gate on the Brighton road. The third emerged to the south at the gate of the priory which had been built on a subsidiary spur into the floodplain.

*   *   *

In this chapter I have tried to set out my contribution to *Beginnings*, and to explain the theories and the practice on which it is based. My purpose has been to argue that teachers can only have full control over their curriculum if they are willing to select and predigest the materials from which their pupils will learn. A textbook must always to some degree destroy the autonomy of the teacher of history. I have suggested that these materials are often best assembled in research units so structured that the researcher is faced with a series of meaningful questions to answer from the evidence presented. Those questions should be designed not merely to establish matters of fact but also to encourage the correlation of data and the making of interconnections. Finally I have tried to show that the history of the local parish, town and region can offer a variety of materials for the construction of units fulfilling the purposes which I have outlined.

At the moment the role of local history in many schools is insultingly analogous to the traditional Sunday School treat—an annual liberating romp in the grounds of the nearest ancient ruin after a year's uninterrupted diet of sermonising on politico-theological abstractions. Its potential will only be fully realised when a broad revolution has swept across the entire field of history teaching to engulf the existing *ancien régime* of vicious or clouded aims and turgid methodology. I confidently expect that in that glorious dawn the names of Defoe and Cobbett, or Beresford, Tate and Hoskins, will be found blazoned on the banners of revolution.

*   *   *

Frances Lawrence   *Textbooks*

1 *A Memorial*[1]

THE school history textbook may be likened to the Albert Memorial. The historian, R. G. Collingwood, recalled it in his *Autobiography* as so ugly as to cause him to make a detour in his daily journeys to avoid seeing it. But this same memorial also caused him to ask whether he was looking for qualities it did not possess instead of seeking the questions to which it was an answer. In the near future, if not today, young teachers may be baffled as to how

[1] The latter part of this chapter is based on an unpublished M.A. dissertation (Sussex 1967) entitled *Forms of Bias in History Writing for Schools*. Frances Lawrence.

it was ever believed that the learning and teaching of history could have been developed by such an instrument as the textbook; or how it was possible that a predecessor could recall it as 'the gospel of truth, the compendium of all knowledge, the only complete and infallible guide to the intellectual Valhalla'.[2]

The context in which school textbooks had such 'canonical authority' around the end of the last century is worth recalling and may provide some understanding of their status. In 1899 a committee of the American Historical Association in a review of the study of history in schools noted that in England 'the most noticeable features are a lack of historical instruction, a common failure to recognise the value of history, and a certain incoherence and general confusion'.[3] Although history as a school subject, as developed by Dr Arnold, was to be found in public schools, in elementary and higher elementary schools the subject was rare until after 1875 when it was made an optional 'class' subject on which grants could be earned. 'In 1899 the official returns show that even of schools taking such subjects only about 25 per cent took history . . .'[4] although by 1900 history did gain more acceptance as a subject. Two implications suggest themselves here; that most teachers called upon to teach history would be ill equipped to do so and so textbooks, where available, might have represented a liberation from chanting of facts and copying blackboard work; that in its infancy the subject, for most, was tarred by the payment-by-results brush—for although officially the worst features of the Twice Revised Code came to an end by 1890, old attitudes and practices of teaching for 'demonstrable' results continued long after.

To offset these deficiencies in subject knowledge and methodology, famous educationists lectured and wrote for elementary and secondary teachers-in-training; for example, J. G. Fitch, H.M.I., gave a series of 'lectures on teaching' in the University of Cambridge;[5] he explained the history textbook problem thus, 'Nothing is easier than to begin by denouncing the school books. No doubt they are all more or less unsatisfactory yet it is difficult to know how if they honestly fulfil their intended purpose they could be otherwise. They must of course be crammed with facts. . . . The more systematic textbooks will also attempt a classification of the

[2] Board of Education Report 1912-13 (H.M.S.O., pp. 58 to 59). The teacher was recalling student days some thirty years before.

[3] Quoted in James Welton, *Principles and Methods of Teaching* (University Tutorial Press, 1901, p. 221).

[4] Ibid.

[5] Published as *Lectures on Teaching* (C.U.P., 1881).

main facts of each reign, under such heads, as "birth and parentage of the sovereign, eminent men, wars", etc. Now, although this looks methodical . . . it destroys its value as a book to read. . . . In spite however of these drawbacks, the use of textbooks is a necessity if you would avoid vagueness and teach history methodically.'[6] Fitch saw the textbook as an adjunct to good oral work but the principal source of material for exercises, for reading aloud and for the learning of facts. (Fitch was a progressive educator who spoke scathingly of Mangnall and her 'Printed Catechism'. 'It is appalling to think of the way in which whole generations of English girls and boys have been stupified by this book and by others like it.' He deplored that Mangnall's *Questions* 'is still actually in use as a task-book to be learned by heart and that new editions of it are in constant demand'.[7]) As late as 1923 the Board of Education's 'Teaching History' Pamphlet No. 57 is still stressing the importance of the textbook especially for non-specialist teachers, while in 1925 the I.A.A.M. *Memorandum on Teaching History* echoes the theme thus '. . . the book often states a case in clearer style and language than the teacher or pupil is able to employ'.

The shortness of school life may also be seen as contributing to the importance of textbooks. Official and other statements in the late nineteenth century and indeed up to the 1920's often refer to the need for school subjects to lay 'firm foundations' upon which a boy of girl would build in later life when schooldays were over. This building metaphor is still in use in 1927 when the Board of Education's *Handbook of Suggestions* stressed the importance of 'laying foundations', of 'solid study', of the necessity of children 'facing the drudgery' of hard work, and it strikes this warning note: 'It is a fatal error to assume that even a young child is incapable of learning and retaining the facts that he will need when he begins to build up and comprehend the structure of history as a whole.'

This stress on 'firm foundations' which a factual textbook could supply is best seen not only against a short school life and the system of 'Half-Timers' which lingered until 1918, but also against the even larger problem of irregular attendance. Children were absent from school for a huge variety of 'reasons' such as bad weather, no change of clothes, being mother substitutes, impassable roads, epidemics, race meetings and the demands of other seasonal

[6] Ibid., pp. 371-72.
[7] Ibid., p. 142. On Mangnall, see the beginning of the fourth section of this volume.

work in which unskilled child labour was traditional.[8] In short, there was a not unimportant belief that there was more 'useful' and important work for a child to do in the 'real' world than at school. For example, in a debate on the 1906 Education Bill, Sir Carne Rasch (M.P. for Essex Chelmsford) said: 'I am here simply as an Agricultural Member, principally to keep the rates down, and particularly the rates for education . . . I can never understand why with the galaxy of talent at the disposal of the Education Department, they cannot alter their syllabus or curriculum so that the children shall be taught that which will be of some little use to them in after-life. Why cannot they be taught the difference between barley and oats, a mangold wurzel and a turnip? . . . An agricultural labourer's children, when they leave school, know little of the practical work of life. . . . Would it not be possible if you modified the curriculum in schools to allow the agricultural labourer's child to leave school a little earlier? An agricultural labourer is not a rich man, and an extra sixpence a week means a good deal to him, and there is no reason why he should not get it if the curriculum is modified and made to include useful work.

'We do not object to education. We can stand a certain amount of it and we respect the prejudices of our well-meaning neighbours and friends but we do not want to be ruined by it in our agricultural districts.'[9]

In the light of these circumstances perhaps the stress on the drudgery of subjects and rote learning may be seen less as a penance and more as a protection for children; to emphasise the grind and the need for 'essential foundations' was perhaps to ensure that education was as hard (and therefore as acceptable) as any juvenile employment; in this way the conventions of the age were used not only against, but by, educationalists.

2 Textbooks and Theories of Learning

Metaphors are a means of inviting comparisons and metaphors used to describe the 'mind', such as 'storehouse' or 'process', demand appropriate verbs such as 'to stock' or 'to enrich'; it is not intended to criticise such metaphors for it is evident that to describe mind and learning *some* metaphor or other must be employed. But upon how it is believed that children learn will depend how they are taught—by educators at any rate—and the ascendancy of

[8] For a useful investigation of conditions in rural schools, see C. Griggs, 'The Development of Elementary Education in a Rural Area, 1870-1914' (unpublished M.A. Thesis, University of London, 1969).
[9] Parl. Debates, 4th Series. Vol. 156, 10th May 1906, col. 1562-64.

faculty psychology at the end of the nineteenth century and beyond throws some light upon the standing of the textbook. If it is believed, as was the case, that the mind is a storehouse, then stocking it is clearly the business of education. Fitch's dictum that a textbook should be 'crammed with facts' carries an explanation different from that already offered. Simple repetition, drills, complicated strategies such as dates painted on ceilings, nonsense rhymes, etc., were necessary and respectable rote-learning methods. The whole range of data which late Victorian and Edwardian children learned — dates of kings and queens, genealogical tables, battles and wars, capes and bays, model drawings, moral tales, arithmetical tables and the like were seen as necessary storage material. Furthermore, the order in which the mind was stocked was believed to be important, for the Herbartian belief in 'classificatory efficiency' by which items could be found quickly 'like books in a well arranged library'[10] was followed if not made explicit. It was generally held that the stockpiling was best achieved by adding the general to the particular, the complicated to the simple, the abstract to the concrete; in other words the data to be stored were seen to have certain optimal positions in the layers of knowledge. The effective study of history depended therefore on an accurate chronology, a definite ordering of facts, beginning at the beginning and moving forward in time. Textbooks echo this building metaphor, none more clearly than G. T. Warner and C. H. K. Marten's famous book *The Groundwork of British History*, the second edition (1923) of which contains a 'Chronological Summary of History' on a special insert of blue paper (one wonders if the authors had a blueprint in mind) in which 'history' is divided into sharp periods; time charts and rigid subdivisions reinforce the main theme.[11] The study of history has, during the greater part of the last hundred years, been restricted by the building metaphor and textbooks are its exponents, especially when such an ordering of the past becomes associated with 'examination history'. It seems then as if the status and nature of the textbook has been and will continue to be shaped by current learning hypotheses although there is some evidence which suggests that occasionally the tail has wagged the dog.[12] But in general terms it is the case that the structure of textbooks is a function of learning theories.

[10] H. M. Felkin and E. Felkin, *An Introduction to Herbart's Science and Practice of Education* (Heath, 1895, p. 115).

[11] Another textbook series entitled 'The House of History' consisted not of volumes but four 'Storeys' (Nelson, 1930-32).

[12] See p. 118, n[24].

3 *Examinations, Howlers and Myths*

The doctrine of the 'examinability' of knowledge which has shaped so many aspects of our education system during the last one hundred and fifty years has impinged upon the study of school history. In the latter part of the nineteenth century, 'the grind' in elementary and higher schools and training colleges, and its counterpart 'the cram' in public schools were structural parts of education. It is more difficult to explain than to describe the peculiar strength of the belief in examinability which held (and still holds) so many teachers and administrators. Edmond Holmes, H.M.I., one of those who had been deeply involved in the system of Payment by Results and who repented his part in its maintenance, reflected: 'The Western belief in the efficiency of examinations is a symptom of a widespread and deep-seated tendency— a tendency to judge according to the appearance of things, to attach supreme importance to visible "results", to measure inward worth by outward standards'.[13] Upon this outward appearance of children's knowledge as assessed by inspection and examination rested such matters as grants-in-aid, selection, promotion and other good things—or the reverse—for schools, teachers, and children; neither were public schools or universities outside these arrangements, whose origins have been traced to both the Benthamite methods for factory, Poor Law and public health inspection,[14] and by a different formulation, to a tradition of ecclesiastical 'visitation'.[15] But whatever the origin, it seems fairly accurate to claim that, from the latter half of Victoria's reign, and well into this century, the examination system was seen as a means of testing not only knowledge but also character.

The progressive and in some ways quite revolutionary educator J. G. Fitch put the case for examinations thus: 'It is good for us, all through life to have in reserve the power of putting special energies into our work at particular emergencies'.[16] Although Fitch deplored 'dishonest preparation, hasty and crude study', yet competent examiners could easily detect these faults. 'We must of course', he said, 'abstain from needless and irritating questions, but we may not forget that, with a child, to leave him unquestioned and untested is not to give better room for the spontaneous exercise of his

---

[13] E. G. A. Holmes, *What Is and What Might be* (Constable, 1911, p. 9).
[14] See J. Leese, *Personalities and Power in English Education*, Chapter I, 'Jeremy Bentham and "Inspectability"' (E. J. Arnold, 1950).
[15] E. L. Edmonds, *The School Inspector* (Routledge, 1962).
[16] J. G. Fitch, op cit., p. 180.

own faculties, but simply to encourage stagnation and forgetful-ness'.[17]

The belief in examinability of school subjects coincided with the growing importance of the textbook—even at the expense of the teacher and well might that young student recall it as 'the compendium of all knowledge' whose contents were to be committed to memory for the prudential reason of examination success. Since those days, although official reports from Spens onwards have lamented the fact that despite all safeguards public examinations 'have dominated the work of [secondary] schools, controlling both the framework and the content of the curriculum' no attempt to date has been notably successful in dislodging the public examination from its mighty judgement seat.

Textbooks are in a symbiotic-like relationship with the system and some examiners' comments on General School Certificate and General Certificate of Education answers at 'O' level between 1918 and 1966[18] provide an important perspective on the influence of textbooks upon the candidates' historical understanding. Running through the reports like a continuous and uniform thread are comments about 'wonderful feats of memory' and 'disastrous attempts to reproduce textbook summaries or notes'; examiners continue to note original interpretations of textbook 'explanations'; for example in the 1956 report—'more wild—or facetious statements than usual . . . "The Saar—a well-meaning ruler of Russia; the Workhouse Test—a stiff exam which had to be passed by a man before he could enter a workhouse" '. In 1966 the Examiners *open* their report with a candidate's howler, 'Thistlewood was very proud of the fact that he was the last man ever executed', and they continue 'this is not an untypical example of the failure of candidates to think for themselves'. The origin of his howler might well have been an adolescent's interpretation of a passage from a very popular textbook—'Thistlewood himself enjoyed the distinction of being the last man in England to be beheaded'.[19]

Although theories of learning and teaching change and notions of 'training' give way to 'education', the examination howler retains its perennial nature. Whether the reason for this is that while theories change, a child's level of understanding of adult textbook explanations does not (a Piagetian-type investigation into history examination howlers would perhaps yield some interesting

[17] Ibid., p. 179.
[18] University of London Examination Reports. Collections at the Library.
[19] D. Richards and J. W. Hunt, *An Illustrated History of Modern Britain* (Longman, 1950, p. 105).

answers, i.e. an enquiry into wrong answers), or whether the howler is a function of the examination system, is problematic. But it would, for example, be difficult to date the following passage with any certainty—'The howlers made by schoolboys and the marvellous answers given in examination papers afford us all much food for mirth from time to time. Funny as they are, there is also pathos in these mistakes . . . they illustrate the utter futility of cramming a child's mind. . . .' There follow some examples of childish interpretations—'"Stafford ruled the people with an iron bar". To his imagination an iron bar was much more appealing than "a rod of iron". . . . Another child of the same calibre peopled the North of Europe with "Esquimaux and Archangels". . . . His companion who considered that the letters of the alphabet were divided into "continents and bowels" had evidently got into a very slough of muddledom . . . which caused him also to think that "subjects had power to partition the King" [and] the youth who held that " 'The Compleat Angler' was another name for Euclid because he wrote all about angles". . . . [He] knew a thing or two and was not as innocent as he would have us believe'.[20]

As well as howlers, there are the myths that arise from the text-book summary or truncated version of events. The textbook author by the very nature of his task is obliged to use generalisations and abridgements which leave the young reader with many strange and often outmoded notions. (A typical comment by examiners on the latter problem was made in 1961: 'The examiners wish the History they read in examination scripts today was less closely bound to the standard interpretations of over 30 years ago . . . they would like to be in a better position to distinguish between the inaccuracies devised by the candidates and those they have acquired from else-where', and, in 1964, examiners expressed concern at 'having to give credit to interpretations of well-known topics that have long been discarded by reputable historians'). Professor Butterfield describes the myths that can arise from abridged history as 'academic dream impressions'[21] of what statesmen, common men and governments can accomplish; some examples of these the London University Examiners (of 'O' level history scripts on nineteenth-century history) discover in their 1961 report: 'In marking the popular sections, examiners are annually compelled to inhabit a twilight world where history becomes barely distinguishable from myth . . . where Palmerston is primarily a bully and a buffoon who

[20] C. M. Spender, 'Blunders in Examination Papers', *Journal of Education*, vol. XXX (Jan.-Dec.), 1908, pp. 603-4.
[21] H. Butterfield, *History and Human Relations* (Collins, 1951, p. 176).

nevertheless brought about the downfall of Louis Philippe by refusing "to lift a little finger to help him". . . where Haussmann rebuilt Paris between 1849 and 1851 . . . where the French had no part at all in the events leading to the war of 1870. . . . Candidates', they complain, 'are not only the slaves of their notebooks; they are also enslaved to the textbook'.[22]

But examiners tend to be ambivalent; on the one hand they complain of 'the bewildering consequences' that follow even the simplest exercise in elementary historical judgement and seem to long for fresh thoughtful answers; but on the other hand they have been content to rely on the well-worn range of clichés that serve as examination questions at this level[23] — clichés that suggest an unholy alliance with textbook 'arrangements' of history. Indeed the charge that examination questions conform to those topics common to the standard textbooks seems a rather Kafka-like suggestion, but it was made in a most unusual report.[24] The report included a swingeing attack on textbooks and it deplored the fact that there seemed to be '"a gentleman's agreement" that questions shall conform to the topics common to standard textbooks'—topics which it detailed as political, constitutional and diplomatic. As well as these restrictive tendencies, the length of the periods for examination leave the teacher 'in bondage to the textbook, the whole textbook and nothing but the textbook' and indeed 'the mass of scripts affords convincing evidence that the reproduction of lifeless textbook formulae . . . deadens the pupil's interest'. Suggestions were made for change but instead of textbooks being banished from the field they had dominated for so long, they merely expanded their demesne to include the new social, economic and cultural 'requirements'. Why textbooks were able to survive this attack is probably best explained by noting that the pages of the Council's leaflet still resound with what in effect was the *rationale* for textbooks—candidates ought to have a knowledge of 'the alphabet 'of history, and ought to leave school 'with a permanent knowledge of the bare framework of history'.

So the argument against textbooks proved to be barren and what promised to be a liberation was not possible and one suspects will

[22] Experienced 'O' level teachers would have no difficulty in tracing the origin of these myths!

[23] Just as difficult as dating howlers is the task of dating examination questions over the last fifty years.

[24] Secondary Schools Examination Council, 'The School Certificate Examination. A Report to enquire into 8 approved School Certificate Examinations held in the Summer 1931' (H.M.S.O., 1931).

not be possible until all themes of frameworks and structures are abandoned as the ends of historical education; neither will textbooks be displaced from their alliance with examinations. Whatever the direction new modes of examining and assessment may take, textbooks will follow where they lead and if 'memorable'[25] and 'mythical' history are cast out, then the textbooks which record such history will also disappear. If 'nothing is more revealing of the purpose underlying a course of study than the nature of the examination given at its close',[26] similarly one might judge the direction of school history by some glances at the textbooks that have, in the past at any rate, sustained it.

4 *Reflections on some History Textbooks for Schools*

Teaching history as a means of teaching something else has a long and respected tradition in our schools, and perhaps the influence of Dr Arnold still casts its long shadow on this subject more than on any other secular study in the curriculum.

This tradition of moralising to child readers is as vigorous as in Dr Arnold's day, whatever 'historiographical stance' an author might find himself in. From the end of the nineteenth century to 1914 Oman and Warner and Marten were recording history as a structure and Britain as the master builder; between the World Wars, in works by Trevelyan, Fawcett and Kitchin and Rayner, history was depicted as the growth of humanity in knowledge and wisdom; later in the 1950's and 1960's the textbooks of Richards and Hunt, and Reed-Brett were recording history as an inevitable movement towards One World. Whatever the stance, these authors whose publications span some sixty years, are united by an activity more powerful than these differences. This activity is the weaving of schoolmasterly injunctions into texts that purport to be about the historical past—injunctions about 'virtues' such as industry, obedience, duty and prudence, and 'evils' such as slackness, extravagance, ignorance, impetuosity and idleness. Today the moralising is less blatant but no less insistent than that of Victorian texts which now are seen as reprehensible or amusing. But this is not to suggest that these moral messages are insinuated by means of a deliberate misrepresentation of the evidence (i.e. at the expense of 'truth'); rather that this particular sort of 'bias' seems inevitable in history texts written for the young. In this activity the study of the past

[25] 'History is not what you thought. It is what you can remember'; so runs the classic denunciation of memorable history in *1066 and All That*.

[26] Alexander Meiklejohn quoted in F. R. Leavis, *Education and the University* (Chatto & Windus, second edition, 1948, p. 44).

seems inextricably mixed with eulogising or deploring. Indeed, the introduction of value judgements in the writing of history is most generally held to be unavoidable and a different act from deliberate falsification of the evidence;[27] or as the historian E. L. Woodward explained over thirty years ago when answering the questions as to whether judgements of good or bad, right or wrong ought to be made by the historian—'. . . the real problem about bias arises not from dishonesty but interpretation and introducing value judgement in the very process of collecting evidence. One's view of what is important and relevant in the past is determined by one's view of what is important in the present'.[28]

In what follows the 'historical past' referred to above is taken as British history, domestic, imperial and foreign, in the nineteenth century—a period which is the most popular period studied for the first public examination (G.S.C. to G.C.E. 1918 to 1967). This is the common context. The textbooks to be discussed were all borrowed from secondary school stock cupboards; a further criterion of the choice was that all have been reviewed in journals for history teachers. An attempt has been made to select books which appear to be addressed to different 'sorts' of children, i.e., public school boys, secondary modern girls and boys. Some of these textbooks such as those by Oman, Rayner or Richards and Hunt are 'household' names to generations of teachers and scholars but in this study a text such as Fawcett and Kitchin is as interesting as a best seller— if only to offer reasons for its being relatively unknown.

(A) Sir Charles Oman's 'Cataclysmic History' (a review of *England in the Nineteenth Century*[29])

This textbook, first published in 1899, was revised and enlarged in 1902 and several 'revised reprints' followed until the last in 1921. That it was a widely used textbook, up until the 1920's at least, is clear, and the popularity of *1066 and All That* may have rested on the fact that so many of those who enjoyed it had been initiated into 'memorable history' by Oman.[30] Further evidence of the

[27] And a different idea from that of Professor Pollard's description of textbooks —'rehashes of old facts flavoured with an original spice of error'.

[28] E. L. Woodward. 'Bias in the Teaching of History at Public Schools' in *History*, vol. XIX, December 1934.

[29] The text used here is a 'revised reprint of the second edition 1902 containing the publishers date 1929'. Edward Arnold Ltd. were unable to say exactly how many reprints there had been but 'it is certain there were quite a few' (extract from a letter from the publishers 9.6.69).

[30] 'Absit Oman' is the dedication of this classic skit on school history by W. C. Sellar and R. J. Yeatman (Methuen, 1930) which, in two years, had run through 15 editions.

influence of this particular way of writing history is that a vast number of textbooks follow having 'Omanesque' overtones—overtones which are distorted echoes of Dr Arnold's beliefs. This traditional way of perceiving history may best be characterised as 'cataclysmic'—Oman's own description. In this particular textbook the history of England in the nineteenth century is seen as one of ever-threatening catastrophe and the country moves in a world of menace and danger. All foreigners are suspect and untrustworthy and there is a persistent association of the word 'enemy' with adjectives such as 'reckless', 'fanatical', 'unbalanced', 'frantic', 'treacherous' and 'malicious'. That Oman found his world a very hostile place is certain; neither were his enemies to be found only beyond his own country. The Irish, Romantic Poets, The Prince Regent, recipients of charity, Trade Unionists and revolutionaries and indeed all troublesome or discontented minorities excite his apprehension, as a few extracts may show:

THE IRISH: 'The widespread plans of the Fenians ended everywhere in ludicrous failure' (p. 160). There follows a description of Fenian incidents using such terms as 'hair-brained [sic] scheme', 'murderous attempts of a gang of desperadoes' (p. 161), and 'The disease of Fenianism' (p. 163).[31]

ROMANTIC POETS (Byron and Shelley): '. . . the one was too morbid and satanic, the other too hysterical and anarchic for the taste of the time' (p. 55). 'Shelley was . . . an active apostle of political and moral anarchy. . . . The most futile and extravagant doctrines of the French school had a fatal attraction for his high-strung and hysterical mind . . .' (p. 119).

THE PRINCE REGENT (the order of the vices is significant): 'But the Regent was frankly disreputable. . . . A debauchee and gambler, a disobedient son, a cruel husband, a heartless father, an ungrateful and treacherous friend . . . (p. 59).

CHARITY: (The Speenhamland System): '. . . this blind philanthropy' (p. 86).

(The Paupers): 'It is impossible to get rid of the tradition of un-thrift and recklessness caused by forty years of maladministration' (p. 87).

(The Workhouse System): '. . . the curse of pauperism was lifted from those of the rural poor who had the strength and in-dependence to fight for themselves. They were no longer compelled to live on charity, the most demoralising of all manners of life' (p. 87).

[31] See D. Richards and John Hunt on 'the infection' and 'contagion' of Communism.

In similar language, Oman condemns all acts of disorder, slackness, recklessness, lax morals, extravagance and idleness. For him the qualities to be most admired are order, firmness, obedience, thrift and independence. War, he believed, could exercise 'a most wholesome and sobering influence upon the national character' (p. 53). In describing alien peoples there is that lack of universalisation of judgement which was, and often still is, so marked a characteristic of other textbook writers, and which in the pithy description by Sellar and Yeatman meant that Britain was 'Top Nation'.

NON-EUROPEANS receive short shrift—The Emancipated Slaves: 'The emancipation . . . was an absolutely necessary act of elementary morality. But . . . the freed men were idle and disorderly; when the fear of the lash was removed they did not take kindly to work. The sugar plantations . . . have been gradually ruined by inefficient free labour [because] the free blacks refuse to carry on systematically' (p. 88). 'The Aborigines of Australia . . . were among the lowest and most barbarous of mankind' (p. 245).

The Indians (in 1900) . . . 'serious riots show from time to time that the British bayonet is still needed to keep the peace. The cheap education which we have lavished upon our subjects . . . has created a half-educated literary proletariat . . .' (p. 239).

The Afghans: 'Any ruler maintained on his throne by British bayonets is bound to be unpopular among the wild and fanatical tribes of Afghanistan' (p. 223).

The Chinese: 'The governor of Canton, acting with the usual stupid arrogance and obstinacy of Chinese officials . . .' (p. 141).

The Suez Canal: '. . . the control of the traffic was entirely in the hands of a grasping French company and a thriftless and oppressive Oriental despot' (p. 172).[32]

Europeans are described in terms such as blasphemous, unscrupulous, intriguing and others which denote excessive bad faith.

The virtues put before children by Oman are clear and few.

Firstly, PATRIOTISM: 'The great [Napoleonic] war had exercised

[32] Two modern interpretations of this view are, in 1950, in Richards and Hunt —'the spendthrift Ismail' and in Reed-Brett in which Ismail's extravagances are repeated as the cause of Dual Control in Egypt. A modern 'African' interpretation is rather different. 'Ismail improved trade, education . . . harbours, docks, railways' and the terms of the loans he contracted 'was excessively profitable to financiers. . . . Then creditors asked Ismail for their "pound of flesh".' Ed. J. C. Anene and G. Brown, *Africa in the Nineteenth and Twentieth Centuries* (Nelson, 1966).

a most wholesome and sobering effect on the national character' (p. 53). 'The best, probably that could be said for the Crimean War was that it taught us to know some of the worst points of our military organisation and raised the spirit of national patriotism which had tended to sink low during the long peace since Waterloo' (p. 139). 'In the spirit of national solidarity each member of the great British family made its fellows' quarrels its own. The splendid future of 1914 might be foreseen' (p. 286).

And secondly, RESPECTABILITY: Victoria; 'The exemplary sovereign . . . the most blameless ruler that Great Britain has ever seen . . . the pattern and model for all constitutional sovereigns . . . who was conspicuously free from all the hereditary faults of her family. . . . She gave the world an example of perfect domestic happiness. To those who remembered the court of George IV, the change made in a few years was quite remarkable' (p. 91).

Parnell and the O'Shea Divorce Suit; 'Public opinion in England has got beyond the stage in which a notorious evil-liver can be accepted as leader of a great party. . . . The Catholic priesthood threw its powerful influence into the scale of morality' (p. 196).

What counted as morality was never in doubt to Oman; he saw life in sharp, irreconcilable alternatives for he had a deep-rooted fear of tolerance in any form. It is tempting to dismiss Oman as a paradigm of an 'authoritarian personality' but this will not do: for Oman was not an exception but *primus inter pares*, the founder of a large school of history writers. Although it is true to say that Oman's views were more common among the educated upper classes at the turn of the century than they are today, nevertheless his successors all share to some degree his *penchant* for moralising to children in the very process of writing about the past.

Yet Oman's excellence in his own specialist field (on the art of war in the Middle Ages) and his pre-Freudian honesty remain; neither did he see himself as a prophet—a role so often assumed by modern textbook authors—but knew that 'It is no doubt a disheartening thought to remember that twenty to thirty years hence . . . our own books on History must go to the limbo of forgotten things. . . . We must think ourselves happy if they appear to our grandchildren rather as glimpses of the obvious than as expositions of exploded heresies. Our work must perish but it had to be done.'[33]

[33] Sir Charles Oman, *Colonel Despard and Other Studies* (Edward Arnold, 1922).

(B) Warner and Marten's History for Public School Boys (a review of *A Groundwork of British History*)[34]

Warner, teaching at Harrow, and Marten, at Eton, were the co-authors of this 'one of the most used school textbooks of the first half of the Twentieth Century'[35] and the latter teacher had the honour of 'being entrusted by King George VI with the historical education of the Princess Elizabeth'.[36] The book under review represents the orthodox public school view of history. Throughout the text is the assumption of values shared between author, teacher and schoolboy—of playing the game, of the rights of property owners and gentlemen, of the necessary example of the ruling classes in conducting the affairs of Britain and her Empire, and of the real intimacy and effectiveness of belonging to a special class. 'The most striking feature of British political life has been that, at all events till recent years, what may be called the public school class has governed Britain'[37] and the footnote on that page reads: 'In the Parliament of 1865 one quarter of the members, it has been computed, were connected with thirty-one families, whilst in the Parliament of 1900, one quarter of the members had been educated at Eton or Harrow'. The names and old school connexions of Cabinet Ministers are sometimes given in as much detail as their achievements in office. LORD PALMERSTON (that magic mirror for textbook authors who find in his character exactly the model for schoolboys they seek) is 'a thorough English gentleman . . . a good humoured and good tempered man, bluff and hearty, loving a political fight and yet a generous foe . . . an excellent landlord and a keen sportsman who made of his exercise as he said "a religion"'[38] and 'somewhat boisterous and truculent, and was perhaps too careless of other nations susceptibilities'. In view of the wide use of this book, it may be wondered what working class children in the L.E.A. secondary schools made of this portrait.

The working classes are definitely 'the others' in this textbook. CHILD LABOUR IN THE COAL MINES: '. . . moreover children in mines were often . . . dragging, tied by girdle and chain on hands

[34] First published in 1911, there were four reprints by 1923; added to but not otherwise altered and published in 1943 by Blackie & Sons as G. T. Warner, C. H. K. Marten and D. E. Muir, *The New Groundwork of British History* (The New Warner and Marten).

[35] D.N.B., 1941-50, p. 577.

[36] Ibid.

[37] G. T. Warner and C. H. K. Marten, *The Groundwork of British History* (Blackie, 2nd edition, 1923, p. 611).

[38] Ibid., p. 627.

and knees, loads of coal unduly heavy for them'.[39] The ordering of the following sentence, in view of the tone of the book, is not unimportant: 'At the same time the fact that men were growing more humane is shown in the first attempts to prevent cruelty to dumb animals, and in the prohibition of spring guns and man-traps. . . .' In the details of pauper relief an interesting yardstick is used; 'or put in another way . . . the cost of such relief is nearly half that of the army'.[40] Considering the emphasis put in this book upon army exploits, especially in the Empire (i.e. domestic history, excluding Ireland, occupies some 20 pages, and the story of the Empire and military events in it occupies some 43 pages) it is possible that Warner and Marten believed this amount was unduly lavish.

In European affairs, England moves as *deux ex machina* and Palmerston is represented as the competent saviour of Belgium, Spain, Portugal and, with some French help, Italy. Francophobia is, however, never far from the surface and their account of the Crimean disasters include French mistakes, a Russian winter, the forgotten art of war, but only a slight suggestion of the incompetence of the British command. The European Powers are condemned for imperialism; in the text, Great Britain *acquired* territory, Russia *ate into* the frontiers of China while Germany *took advantage* of the murder of two missionaries to acquire Kiau-Chau.

But it is the imperial story which best illustrates that belief that British rule will bring justice, peace and stability to inferior peoples. This view as George Orwell pointed out was also the coin in the world of 'Boys' Weeklies': 'The year is 1910—or 1940 but it is all the same. . . . Over in Europe the comic foreigners are jabbering and gesticulating, but the grim grey battleships of the British fleet are steaming up the Channel, and at the outposts of the Empire, the monocled Englishmen are holding the niggers at bay. . . . Everything is safe, solid and unquestionable. Everything will be the same for ever and ever'.[41] Textbooks and the 'Gem/Magnet' stereotypes reinforced each other; for example consider the following of Warner and Marten's views, THE BRITISH OCCUPATION OF EGYPT: '. . . the Khedive could not stand alone and it was clear that, in order not only to reform the country, but to save it from anarchy, some power must interfere. . . . [The occupation] has to the infinite benefit of the country, lasted till this day'.[42] THE

---

[39] Ibid., p. 596. One wonders what weight might have been duly heavy for them.
[40] Ibid., p. 601.
[41] G. Orwell, *Critical Essays* (Secker, 1946, p. 70).
[42] Warner and Marten, op. cit., p. 678.

INDIAN MUTINY: After the treachery and brutality of the 'revolting Sepoys'[43] is described in some detail, 'Stern punishment was meted out to those who deserved it, as the tragedies of the Mutiny, especially Cawnpore, made it impossible for the British to be altogether merciful'.[44] NATIVES OF AFGHANISTAN are (traditionally) 'Sultry and sullen' and these adjectives are but two amongst a considerable array used to register disapproval. Woven into the text are a host of moral injunctions against 'dawdling', 'ignorant sentimentality', 'indiscipline' and 'extravagance'. Gentlemanly restraint, respect for the monarchy and imperial ardour are the golden virtues; the message for the public school boy is clear and seems to have little to do with the book's caption (*Lucem Libris Disseminamus*).

(C) Arcadian History by G. M. Trevelyan, o.m. (a review of *British History in the Nineteenth Century*[45])

An interestingly muted version of Drum and Trumpet history occurs in the work of G. M. Trevelyan and this may be accounted for not so much as a consequence of World War I, but more because of his own literary and cultural interests. By 1928 the book had run through eight impressions and represents a view of a 'country gentleman' writing in a free-flowing and gracious style a nostalgic history in praise of that class he believed represented an unbroken link with the pre-industrial past—'Most of us would be at home taking tea at Dr Johnson's, hearing the contact of civilised men with society discussed. . . . Only we should be aware that we had stepped out of a scientific, romantic and mobile era into an era literary, classical and static'.[46] Reviewing the book in 1923, Elie Halévy praised its 'liberal and scrupulously judicial though patriotic treatment' of foreign affairs and especially those sections dealing with Napoleon III and Bismarck as 'masterpieces of quiet and high-minded impartiality'.[47] Today the book seems less unbiased, but instead an eulogy of 'British commonsense and good nature, British idiosyncrasy and prejudice'[48] and the virtues of his people he, too, finds in Lord Palmerston—'zest, nonchalance and courage. But with all his faults it was owing to him to his generosity and open speech that Britain's name was associated with the cause of freedom. . . .'[49] 'There was in him much of the aristocrat, but nothing of the snob'.[50]

---

[43] As a teacher of history, the author was delighted to find the origin of this favourite howler.   [44] Op. cit., p. 694.

[45] Longman. First Edition, 1922. Reprint, 1928.   [46] Ibid., p. xiv.

[47] *History*, vol. vii, Jan. 1923.   [48] G. M. Trevelyan, op. cit., p. xvi.

[49] Ibid., p. 297.   [50] Ibid., p. 299.

In Trevelyan's representation of the monarchy in his *cri-de-coeur* for serenity that institution is depicted as a haven against disquiet —'Queen Victoria . . . made the world recognise in her the symbol of all that was mighty and lasting in the life of England and of the races associated with England in Empire. . . . As the little grey figure passed in her carriage . . . there was a sense that we had come into port after a long voyage. But in human affairs there is no permanent haven and we are forever setting out afresh across new and stormy seas'.[51]

To Trevelyan to be British is to inherit a tradition which no foreigner can really understand; to build an Empire is to bestow on less fortunate races the blessings of good government and a superior culture. The extension of the Empire is represented as a civilising mission and the story rolls over on conquest, annexation and reprisal with this as an over-riding justification. In Chapter XX on India, the 'noble traditions' of 'the Civil Service organised rule for the benefit of the Indians' and 'Pax Britannica gave peace and justice novel to Indian states' although he regrets that after the Mutiny 'it was difficult to restore the sense of "glad confident morning" again'.[52] Or, in describing the Partitioning of Africa (that affair which so troubles historians today) as 'full of romantic adventure' he says, 'It was a great triumph for the principles of peace and negotiation'[53] and 'Darkest Africa had become ripe for white control. . . . As among the nations of Europe, Britain had the greatest share of Africa. . . . On the whole that has proved very fortunate for the African.'[54]

Discomforting events of the nineteenth century are defused and rendered harmless. The disasters of the Crimean War are turned to patriotic purposes—'Fortunately the splendid regimental traditions . . . remained to save us in the Crimea and to be transmitted with fresh honours—the names of Alma and Inkerman . . . to keep alive in the records of the regiments the soul of an army not accustomed to yield'.[55] Novel ideas which might prove discomforting are, consciously or unconsciously, anglicised. 'Socialism may be said to have been invented in England by Robert Owen and

---

[51] Ibid., p. 423.   [52] Ibid., p. 322.   [53] Ibid., p. 411.

[54] Ibid., p. 412. It is interesting to compare this view with that of J. C. Anene (who puts his metaphors to a different purpose) in *Africa in the Nineteenth and Twentieth Centuries*. 'The significance of the Partitions need not be exaggerated. . . . In most of Africa therefore European control lasted a mere 60 to 80 years, and in the ocean of History, that is but a wave breaking on the shore'. According to Anene and Brown the most useful legacy of the Europeans (in E. Africa) is the railways.   [55] Ibid., p. 305.

some of his later contemporaries'[56] and, 'The idealism which was abhorrent to the true Marxist materialist was upheld by the poet and author William Morris', and 'Fabians exonerated Socialists from the heavy duty of reading Marx'.[57] 'The Red Cross Movement all over the world starting from the Geneva Convention of 1864, was the outcome of 'her [Florence Nightingale's] work and influence'.[58]

Trevelyan sees the Franco-Prussian War in Chapter XXII as a threatening cloud over his serene English landscape—a cloud he suggests that could have been dispersed—if Napoleon III had not been stricken by 'physical weakness and moral apathy'; if he had waited until Austria had recovered; if he had 'paid Italy her price of Rome as capital', if Great Britain had not been so ignorant of Germany and instead had heeded those 'eccentric intellectuals like Matthew Arnold and George Meredith', who 'warned us that there was something in German professors and their *geist* that was at once admirable and dangerous'.[59] These particular reflections seem to arise from Trevelyan's sense of the pity of it all, for the victory of Prussia was to him the victory of the dark forces of 'race hatred', 'race war and class war' and 'Power began to replace justice as the standard of international appeal'.[60] Coupled with this view is Trevelyan's belief that Britain was 'coldly neutral' and superior to the whole tragic affair. 'There was no question of interference. England had no wish to fight.'[61] Similarly he explains Britain's decision not to challenge the Russian entry to the Black Sea, 'But we could not fight for an arrangement which we felt to be of doubtful justice'[62] (i.e. the 1856 Black Sea Clauses of the Treaty of Paris).

But it seems that Trevelyan protests too much, and some thoughts disturb him which must be stifled for fear they shatter that 'quiet and high minded impartiality' (which Halévy found so admirable) and that reconciliation of the disquieting 'scientific and mobile' twentieth century with the literary and classical tradition which his recounting of history had created.

(D) History with the Wars Left Out (a review of *The World Today*, by E. N. Fawcett and M. le S. Kitchin)

In looking at textbooks written between the Wars it is difficult to be sure if all authors found the Great War completely regrettable. A certain ambivalence also occurs in official opinion—for

[56] G. M. Trevelyan, op. cit., p. 402.   [57] Ibid., p. 403.   [58] Ibid., p. 307.
[59] Ibid., p. 363.   [60] Ibid., p. 366.   [61] Ibid., p. 364.
[62] Ibid.

example in the Board of Education's *Suggestions for 1927*. Although history syllabuses ought to be widened, yet Our Island Story is still of premier importance (if to be told less aggressively); it recomments a useful and apparently non-controversial theme 'The Progress of Science' which 'should be impressed on the pupils'. Certainly the metaphor of history as a 'natural growth' or progress is gaining ascendancy at this time ('Lines of Development' themes are popular in history syllabuses); perhaps this was because these notions were entering into the language via the biological sciences or perhaps it was an attempt to erase from the mind the possibility that the course of history might have been different; 'Inevitable Growth' theories can be comforting, removing awful doubts and lessening a sense of choice and responsibility.

A textbook which utilises uncontroversial and natural progress themes, and shows only covert suspicion of foreigners is *The World Today*, by E. N. Fawcett and M. le S. Kitchin.[63] The characteristic of this book is that it presents history with the wars left out as well as minimising or ignoring all domestic, foreign and imperial controversies. Even Lord Palmerston, the beloved hero of most authors, is absent for he represented 'swaggering nationalism',[64] an attitude which cannot be reconciled with history as interpreted by these authors—history in praise of science and technology where men do not pit themselves against each other but against disease, illiteracy and the elements. Men are depicted as building bridges not Empires and the rewards are material ones.

History as illustrated by bridge-builders, bankers, inventors and factory owners points a lesson; namely that all things work together for the good of an Englishman who is thrifty, persistent, honest and ambitious. For whom are the great men[65] of the text—Lister, Wedgwood, Watt, the Rothschilds—to be the models? Clearly not for public school boys who are presented with a quite different array of heroes in Drum and Trumpet histories. It appears that the future skilled working class are addressed and enlightened as to the good intentions of all men, especially Big Business, Bankers and Governments. In a chapter entitled 'The Nineteenth Century from Three Angles', one angle is 'The Rothschilds and Banking: Big

[63] Volume VII in *Collins Biographical Histories* (Collins 1932. First and only edition).

[64] Ibid., p. 317.

[65] Heroes who are common men are increasingly the vogue (*Piers Plowman* had been published in 1922; the Quennells' work in 1918) in the 1930's; and abroad there was the publication in 1924 of George Lefebvre's studies of the French peasantry during the Revolution.

I

Business'. The authors believe that the growth of 'these giant businesses' is 'on the whole for our benefit'.

Domestic problems are glossed over by a euphemistic flow of words or, sometimes, omissions. For example the Cato Street Conspiracy (that issue which was surrounded with mystery and yet evoked some pretty loud Drum and Trumpet noises) is embraced thus: 'It will be understood then why there was much discontent and why many people were engaged in thinking out reforms or demanding them'.[66] The Poor Law Amendment Act is applauded because 'a wholesome horror of the workhouses turned many "professional paupers" into industrious labourers'.[67] In the sections of the book dealing with Ireland, one never learns the causes of 'the troubles'. Civil war seems to erupt for no reason and famine 'swooped upon her' in 1845. There is also an apparent misrepresentation of the efficacy of the Corn Law repeal by which they claim 'foreign corn poured into the country and released both corn and potatoes for the Irish people',[68] and here the matter rests as if at a successful conclusion. Parnell is made to carry the blame for Irish unrest in the 1880's and 90's — 'a small Wicklow landowner with American rebel blood in him and a Fenian mother and sister'. The impression left is that the Irish are by nature very troublesome and are swayed by 'Cosmic Forces'. The monarchy receives scant mention; Victoria is recorded as opening the Great Exhibition, but doing little else; the Exhibition is dwelt upon at length: 'This was the first of many exhibitions in the capital of Europe [sic], and it opened a new era of international trade and advertisement which acted as a great stimulus to commerce'.[69]

Deliberate attempts are made not to be beastly to foreigners; this is achieved by leaving out the causes and courses of wars, by emphasising, for example, the technological acceleration that the First World War produced, or by presenting wars (i.e., the Indian Mutiny) as troublesome breaks in the march of scientific progress. Brogan's phrase about 'deodorised history' springs to mind over this statement, 'Communism, his [Marx's] plan of state control and sharing profits in common, he proposed as a way out of the difficulty'[70] [of Capital versus Labour].

The growth of the British Empire is seen as offering splendid

[66] E. N. Fawcett and M. le S. Kitchin, op. cit., p. 100.

[67] Ibid., p. 138. Cf this to Oman's notion of charity as 'the most demoralising of all manners of life', see p. 14. This Victorian belief persists well into the twentieth century.

[68] Ibid., p. 302.   [69] Ibid., p. 170.   [70] Ibid., p. 183.

opportunities for trade and its foundation as 'the accidental settling of adventurous traders and the spreading of men in search of new homes'.[71] Britain 'with Daughter Lands and Colonies' is 'an empire bound together by goodwill, a far surer tie than force'. The reasons of those who resist this goodwill are either not examined (i.e., the causes of the Boer War) or are made a cause for a show of mild irritation that there are persons so unenlightened as to be ignorant of the blessings of Western technology. The Indian Mutiny is an irrational interruption of the development of trade, railways and irrigation canals. This tone is slightly disturbed however when Americans attempt the same sort of mission—'For two hundred years Japan dreamt among her cherry blossoms, living up to her part in "the unchanging East". Then she was rudely awakened by a hustling American, Commodore Perry, who in 1853, forced a commercial treaty upon her.'[72] The history of the West Indies is told (unaccountably) as a success story, although the authors are not really sure about the abolition of slavery. After saying that the compensated ex-slave-owners had grounds for discontent, they continue: 'Only the African negro was strong enough to work in that climate and he had no intention of doing so unless he was forced. Even when he could be induced to work for good wages, the planter suffered. . . .'[73] The authors do not sense the dilemma the West Indies presents to their interpretation of history, namely economic decline—not growth—caused by a development of scientific agriculture, i.e. beet sugar.

Finally there is another feature of this book worth noting: nearly all the illustrations are pretty and trivial and are so placed, by accident or design, to face the written descriptions of discomforting events. A picture of three dolls opposes the account of the Speenhamland System, a fashionable evening gown faces the Fenian disorders, and another lady, elegantly attired, looks at the description of the evictions of Irish tenants.

But probably this is by chance and more certain conclusions may be drawn; an adolescent presented with this rosy image of events would be less able to make sense of causes of aggression than a boy or girl nourished on jingoistic history; and it appears that the training of contented workers, not the education of democrats, is the object of this book.

[71] Ibid., p. 87.
[72] Ibid., p. 184.
[73] Ibid., p. 138. Again Oman's judgement on this matter seems strangely similar—'when the fear of the lash was removed they did not take kindly to work . . . the free blacks refuse to carry on systematically'. See p. 122.

(E) Worthwhile History for Examination Purposes (a review of Robert M. Rayner's *England in Modern Times*)

A vastly different sort of history written in the interwar years was that of Rayner, an indefatigable author of textbooks, whose popularity has continued for over forty years. The book to be discussed was first published in 1929, but as recently as 1958 in a review of a new edition of a Rayner text, W. I. Fowler ponders on the reasons for his perennial attraction—especially as his books 'are not quite in line with contemporary views'[74]; he finds his formula includes, 'a fine sense of story telling', 'an evergreen style' and even the occasional slang which irritates examiners: but throughout, Rayner never loses sight of the examination goal (or in the words of a reviewer in 1934, 'serving to remind the boy who is enjoying History, that he must not enjoy himself too much').[75]

What attitudes met with in this book may help to account for the unchallenged popularity of Rayner in many schools—which from the 1930's were concerned more with L.E.A. than public school candidates? It is certain that his liberal (in the Gladstonian sense) notions represent the values of the respectable middle classes rather than public school attitudes. For example, Rayner's ideal man of the nineteenth century is not Palmerston, who carries voters away with his 'bombast'; instead other heroes are raised up and so persuasive is his style that one cannot doubt that these men became at least the officially sanctioned heroes to generations of school children.[76] There is Gladstone, the Christian statesman, inspired by duty not monarchs, the enemy of privilege, corruption and inefficiency in high places—while Irish, Afghans, Sudanese and other subject peoples struggling to be free torment his fine conscience— in short a veritable giant of morality and physique; or there is Gordon that 'brave and able soldier and a high-minded Christian gentleman';[77] or Cecil Rhodes, the millionaire, freelance adventurer who scorned luxury and government assistance alike and sacrificed himself to a noble plan so impetuously betrayed by Dr Jameson.

To Rayner, Newman's categories did not arise, for to be a Christian was to be a gentleman, and a hero is, necessarily, both. The *milieu* that nourishes such men is middle class; disguising his

[74] *History*, vol. XLIII, p. 34.

[75] Ibid., vol. XVIII, 1934, p. 362.

[76] This was my experience; some 25 years after my own 'Raynerization', politically informed persons labelled me 'a Gladstonian liberal at heart'.

[77] R. M. Rayner, *England in Modern Times* (Longman, 1930, p. 372).

own views with the conventional phrase 'many people think', he says 'that Britain never enjoyed such wise and efficient government as during those mid-century years when the old Tory resistance to reform had been broken down, but modern democratic restlessness had not set in'.[78] The upper classes are tinged, if ever so faintly, with decadence who 'stick to old traditions after they have long ceased to have any meaning';[79] and descriptions of lower class unrest are often concluded with the judgement that, whatever their discontents, they are better off in Britain; being of this conviction it is not surprising that Rayner makes no mention of the Tolpuddle Martyrs and the account of Chartist risings is minimised as 'some futile little riots in the Midlands and South Wales'; and it is surely a middle class response to see co-operatives as giving their members 'a bracing sense of "having a stake in the country" and affording experience of working together in a common cause which was a valuable apprenticeship for democracy'.[80] Socialist Utopias are the wild dreams of those who ignore the pecuniary instincts of men; for example, Robert Owen's plan to 'establish communistic settlements where people were to live happy and blameless lives without money and without competition . . . all failed owing to the unfortunate fact, which Owen overlooked, that habits of selfishness have been ingrained in human nature by thousands of years struggling for existence'.[81]

Science and its consequences are kept well in control as the 'Handmaid of Man'; likewise the monarchy seems a shadowy institution and Queen Victoria is at times seen as the butt of Palmerston's high spirits, the willing recipient of Disraeli's compliments but unable to appreciate Gladstone's fine character; above all she is seen as presiding over the splendid achievements of the middle class.

Rayner's judgements on European Powers are suspicious but restrained, for he is nothing if not a realist in his interpretations of foreign policy, and conscious of the smallness of the British Army. The French lack keenness (especially during the Crimean War), the Italians are 'politically backward' and the Germans, by nature, are aggressive.

But it is in dealing with imperial history that Rayner, moving between high moral tone and opportunism, makes some of his most typical judgements. The Empire is 'united by bonds whose strength comes from their "looseness"', or 'the Empire was not gained by conquest . . . was not a result of deliberate policy' but 'a thing of

---

[78] Ibid., p. 251.   [79] Ibid., p. 317.   [80] Ibid., p. 276.   [81] Ibid., p. 273.

organic growth like a tree or a man'.[82] Rayner sees the Empire as 'a consequence of the national character', 'the spirit of adventure and love of personal independence'—'sturdy individualism and traditions of self-government bred in their bones'. Those bones, it seems, must belong to that middle class whose qualities are applauded throughout the book. His bias is more subtle than that of the old masters; while praising English he can, *en passant* damn the others, and he can reconcile high morality with good business sense by which the middle classes can conduct all affairs as Christian gentlemen and still make a profit; (or if they are school children, still pass examinations).

(F) Today's History—I, 'Myths' (a review of *An Illustrated History of Modern Britain* by D. Richards and J. W. Hunt)

Since 1945 the assumption that national history should be viewed either as part of Western European or World history has been implicit in the works of many historians, conferences on teaching history, public examination syllabuses, textbook revision and Official Reports.[83] Wendell Wilkie's slogan that 'we are now all members of one world' acquires considerable status and for textbook authors this normative statement demands new interpretations of British history in the nineteenth century. If nationalism and imperialism are less relevant or acceptable for twentieth century purposes, how can the age of nationalism be interpreted except as modestly or light-heartedly as possible? Another factor in the debunking of nationalism is the rise of psychology; for it appears that nationalism serves many covert purposes. Taken together the influences of the One World doctrine and psychological realism may make the meaning of the nineteenth century uncertain.

A representative textbook (in the sense that its great popularity seems to be based on its accord with current attitudes) is that of Richards and Hunt.[84] This book recounts the national story in

---

[82] The belief that the Empire grew by accident and not by force is according to E. H. Dance 'our special myth'. By 1966 in a D.E.S. Pamphlet No. 51 the Commonwealth has become 'an international idea'.

[83] Examples of this interpretation can be found in (1) P. Geyl, *Use and Abuse of History* (Yale U.P., 1955). (2) G. Barraclough, *An Introduction to Contemporary History* (C. A. Watts, 1964). (3) G. Eckert, 'Textbook Revision' in *The Year Book of Education*, 1960-64. (4) Ministry of Education, 'Teaching History', Pamphlet No. 23 (H.M.S.O., 1952). (5) Ministry of Education, 'Schools and the Common-wealth' (H.M.S.O., 1961). (6) Dept. of Education and Science, 'The Commonwealth in Education', No. 51, 1966. (7) Dept. of Education and Science, 'Towards World History', Pamphlet No. 52 (H.M.S.O., 1967).

[84] D. Richards and J. W. Hunt, *An Illustrated History of Modern Britain* (Longman, 1950).

ostensibly patriotic tones and all the great men—Palmerston, Gladstone, Disraeli and others, are there; the praise rendered to Science is limited by a recognition of its dangers. But there is an element of unreality in the mode of explanation which may have contributed to Examiners' complaints about 'mythical history'.[85]

These authors are confronted by a problem common to all those who today comment about the past: namely it is no longer possible to praise the deeds of famous men and nations wholeheartedly. For Richards and Hunt the solution is a whimsical, half-facetious style; then the hero, the villain, the great and the ignoble deeds of the past can be set in that 'twilight world' where perhaps things are not what they might seem. A reviewer[86] believed that, by its tone, the book lost an opportunity to find common ground with the new generation in the grammar school, but nevertheless found much to praise especially the use of cartoons. The first criticism is to some extent justified, but in the matter of the cartoons—to misquote, 'the meaning of a cartoon is in the company it keeps',[87] and since in this book history is treated with a very light almost indifferent touch, the cartoons reinforce a sense of bathos.[88] The tone of the book is waggish and detached and there is an elusive quality in which the events are slightly unreal (in one section at any rate); the imperial section is couched in more robust, almost Omanesque tones and acts as a foil to the domestic and foreign accounts.

Whimsy is hard to catch, as the following passages show. PETERLOO: 'So the crowd in a holiday spirit, but bearing banners with determined looking devices such as "Votes for All" and "Reform or Death" set off for Manchester'.[89] REFORM RIOTS: '. . . and at Bristol a mob attacked the Tory M.P., sacked the Mansion House and burnt the Bishop's Palace. Order was restored only by the time-honoured cavalry charge'.[90]

CHILD LABOUR: '. . . and because of their parents' poverty or lack of feeling children of four . . . were often driven to toil from early morn to late at night.'[91]

THE POOR: '. . . were less inclined to be passive under their misfortunes than in the past, for elementary education had taught many to read and a few to think.'[92]

---

[85] See p. 117.

[86] L. W. Hearne in *History*, vol. XXXVII, Oct. 1952.

[87] 'The meaning of a word is in the company it keeps', I. de Sola Pool.

[88] In psychological terms it might be argued that cartoons might raise the guilt threshold by treating serious matters as fun.

[89] D. Richards and J. W. Hunt, op. cit., p. 102.   [90] Ibid., p. 120.

[91] Ibid., p. 23.   [92] Ibid., p. 235.

LOUIS NAPOLEON: 'The most interesting of these additions to the forces of law and order [i.e., for the Chartist meeting] was the future Napoleon III who was very appropriately given a beat on Piccadilly.'[93]

PATRIOTIC POEMS: Tennyson 'promptly obliged with an appropriate set of verses'.[94] 'Tennyson of course supplied the appropriate poem.'[95]

IMPERIALISM: '. . . and the sacred obligation to advance the welfare of natives, "The White Man's Burden," could be agreeably combined with empire-building and profit-making'.[96]

In addition to this sort of tone, there is a form of expression which 'defuses' disturbing ideas—not by anglicising events or adopting a lofty tone but a kind of urbanity. For example, they speak of 'the good fortune or merit of Britain'; 'harsh or unwise government'; a history of hostility being 'forgotten or overlooked'; a government 'were given—or created the excuse'.

It is however when these authors are dealing with matters upon which they do feel strongly that this bantering tone becomes rather curious; one learns the nature of communist and/or socialist beliefs only through allusive metaphors such as a 'particular brand of socialism known as Communism'.[97] 'New Zealand has had a larger dose of Socialism than any other English-speaking nation and seems to like it.'[98] Under a Punch cartoon which depicts a ruffian and a gentleman, the authors add the note that this was how 'the great majority of citizens' regarded the Labour Party and 'The Labour ruffian accompanies the harmless old Liberal gentleman. . . . But the brute's intention is only to knock his companion over the head with the cudgel of Socialism and make off with his property.'[99]

Finally this approach produces an original definition of the *cordon sanitaire*—alias Communism.

'Two looming shadows darkened the hopeful prospect [of World Peace in 1918]. One was Communist revolution. . . . The other danger, ally of the first, was . . . hunger and disease. The policy of the victorious Allies towards Russian Communism was first to attempt its overthrow by armed force, and when this failed, to protect Western Europe from its contagion. This they were able to do by recognising the small states which had sprung up along the whole of Russia's western frontier and which the Allies hoped would be a *cordon sanitaire* against the spread of Communist

---

[93] D. Richards and J. W. Hunt, op. cit., p. 173.   [94] Ibid., p. 171.
[95] Ibid., p. 183.   [96] Ibid., p. 238.   [97] Ibid., p. 235.
[98] Ibid., p. 408.
[99] Ibid., p. 237. *Punch* = the Great Majority of Citizens in this neat equation.

infection.'[100] So without overt statement left-wing opinions are associated with a medicine, theft and contagious diseases.

In the imperial section the 'Omanesque' overtones are pronounced. Old favourites such as 'the spendthrift Ismail', Mehemet Ali 'an unscrupulous adventurer', 'the fanatical Sikhs' are there. Neither would Oman have been unhappy with this Maori solution, '[they] finally retained about half of the North Island which was sufficient for their needs after the reduction of their numbers'. Here, too, is to be found our special old myth—and the new one 'She [Great Britain] came "in a fit of absence of mind" as far as the government was concerned to acquire vast territories suited to white settlement. She peopled them with emigrants, became the foremost colonising power, and built up a partnership of nations based on new ideas of freedom and co-operation.'[101]

But leaving aside the traditional Empire story, what do these authors find important for children to know since on a cursory glance nothing seems to engage them deeply? Firstly, that competence and honesty are to be valued: the lack of these qualities are their attributed causes for the failure of such diverse enterprises and institutions as the General Strike, the Indian Mutiny, the Tsarist régime in 1917, the Italian government of 1921, or the clergy reserves in Canada in 1836. In short, incompetence and dishonesty bring disaster. Secondly, they believe that privileges should be bestowed from above, never seized as rights from below and this holds good for electors, trade unions and all who aspire to influence others.

Finally, although they seem not to believe in nineteenth-century history, they believe in schoolboys and this may in part account for the great popularity of their book. Textbook authors find what they seek in Lord Palmerston and Richards and Hunt choose to depict him as a character with whom boys at any rate may identify.[102] For Palmerston is variously 'a card', 'breezy' and 'outspoken' who holds the destinies of Europe in his careless hand; who is the rascal of Europe, who exasperates all governments; he is depicted as a whirlwind of activity, 'riding storms', 'back at his old tricks', 'going too far', and 'retiring shamefacedly' and whether one likens the description of his appetite to that of Billy Bunter or his longevity to that of Peter Pan, to the authors at any rate, Palmerston (and schoolboys) seem 'evergreen'.

---

[100] Ibid., p. 274.　　[101] Ibid., pp. 398-99.
[102] How far this constitutes escapism one cannot tell, but such an interpretation would accord well enough with 'mythical history'.

Today's History—II, 'Objectivity' (a review of S. Reed-Brett's *From George III to George VI*)

The European movement for the revision of textbooks, to eliminate those references either deliberate or accidental which might be harmful to international understanding, made some headway between the wars and has since become a concern of U.N.E.S.C.O. Briefly, the movement seeks to make available to textbook writers certain interpretations of disputed events as agreed on by a range of historians and to discourage stereotyping and devaluing of alien cultures. But such good intentions carry other problems and the textbook[103] chosen to illustrate them, although containing little of the type of prejudice of earlier authors, displays the problems that are inherent in writing 'objective history'. For example in allocating the blame for a war, if every state is attributed with aggressive tendencies, then since the war is the fault of everyone, in a sense it is the fault of no one and a statement like 'war was inevitable' may seem to draw upon the cause of an Irrational Fate.

Another problem is that described by Oman (the least philosophical of historians) — 'Historical facts however cannot be boiled down into a syrup equally satisfactory to all consumers. If such a book could be written . . . it could only be by shirking moral problems . . . an arid waste of hard facts.' Reed-Brett's task of writing objective history is further complicated by his aim of giving a concise summary of events for secondary-modern candidates for the 'O' level examination—candidates for whom this particular examination was never intended.

It is true that the history in this book offers no chance of emotional involvement—there is no burning patriotism, no overt judgement of good or evil, no heroes, no villains, no scandal, excitement or tragedy; events are presented as if nothing else could have happened—as inevitable answers, and the reader is not invited to imagine possibilities. Yet curiously enough the book does not succeed in being unbiased; not only does it hammer home its bias of utility but also it seeks to convey the impression that practically nothing is difficult to understand if only one knows enough facts. For example:

THE VERSAILLES SETTLEMENT: 'It is not difficult for us to look back in the light of later events and be wiser than they [the Peacemakers] were.'[104]

GLADSTONE'S DEFEAT IN 1885: 'As with other matters it is

---

[103] S. Reed-Brett, *From George III to George VI (1760-1952)* (E. Arnold, First Edition, 1959. 7th Reprint, 1965).   [104] *Ibid.*, p. 331.

easy to look back and say what ought to have been done. But how much Gladstone is to be blamed for acting as he did . . . it is difficult to decide.'[105]

By knowing enough facts, it seems to be suggested, by balancing pros and cons like items in a scales, great issues can be decided.

The text has a certain flatness in its explanation which arises because the author chooses to be precise, because he has in mind those secondary-modern pupils whose selection for examination history he notes in his preface was made 'relatively late in their school careers'; and there is 'limited time and scope available for the subject'. The abridging device he employs to avoid lengthy explanations is to categorise complex events as 'strange'.

LORD SHAFTESBURY as the champion of industrial workers: 'Before Parliament was reformed, the factory workers had no vote, so it was not in everyone's interest to champion their cause. . . . All the more strange it was, therefore, than when a workers' champion did arise he was not a worker but a member of an aristocratic family and did not agree with democratic ideas or reforming parliament.'[106]

TRADE UNIONS: 'Strange though it may seem this pioneer Robert Owen was not a factory worker but a factory owner.'[107]

LAISSEZ FAIRE AND THE EMPLOYMENT OF CHILDREN: 'It seems a strange idea for people to hold at a time when the mass of the people were plainly at the mercy of circumstances in which they were not free to seek their own interest.'[108]

THE FASHODA INCIDENT is 'a strange episode'.

Readers might find their history unaccountable as a result of this technique of eliminating explanations.

Another device employed, perhaps for the sake of time and clarity is that events are dealt with in their 'proper place' and hence there is a loss of a sense of interconnectedness. Brett sees every fact having its proper place and the question arises as to the similarities with Ince and Warner and Marten—although the arranging of data may be for different reasons.

Although the book's area of prejudice is much smaller than that of 'the old masters' yet it is clearly present in the section on imperial affairs.[109] The old charges against Ismail's extravagances occur as causes of Dual Control: 'Ismail naturally disliked this interference,

---

[105] Ibid., p. 197.   [106] Ibid., p. 128.
[107] Ibid., p. 211.   [108] Ibid., p. 129.
[109] Here, as in other matters, author's prejudice seems to be in inverse proportion to knowledge of an event. See my Dissertation, *Forms of Bias in History Writing for Schools* (M.A. Sussex, 1967), Ch. 12, 'Some Interpretations of the Cato Street Conspiracy'.

though he had brought it upon himself and did not work smoothly with the commission'. Gordon is still the noble character (although 'rash and immovably obstinate') pitted against 'the fanatical religious fervour of the Mahdists'. Reed-Brett also shared Rayner's cynicism—if not his style—that Utopias are suspect when he says of Owen's community settlements: 'The fact was that he planned them for unselfish, high-minded people and too many of the actual people were selfish and unprincipled'.

There is another thread connecting this to all other school history textbooks reviewed—namely that perhaps unintentional underlining of what the author sees as valuable for children. For Brett these qualities are restraint, discipline and education. Citizens should go about their work quietly. Describing trade unions, their early difficulties are ascribed, among other reasons, to the fact that 'the workers were very ignorant and of course lacked experience of how to choose the right leaders and of the sort of discipline necessary if a struggle with an employer was to be carried through successfully'. Of depressed working-class conditions in the nineteenth century he says: 'These were the conditions which only education and experience could gradually improve'—as if no other factors or no other tempo might be effective.

In one of the few open judgements made in this objective history book, Brett shows his hand in favour of conformity, sobriety of dress and manners for the 'Second Quartile' when he deplores in unusually strong terms the characteristics he singles out for mention about Disraeli—opportunism and flamboyance—'in spite of which he was a great favourite of Queen Victoria'. That there is a possibility that Victoria found Disraeli fascinating, not in spite of, but because of these characteristics seems not to occur to Brett—but then in this book there is no room for the 'delicious truancy of idle thinking'.

So even in objective history Reed-Brett follows the tradition of other textbook authors:—of slipping in a few schoolmasterly commendations for those qualities he believes are valuable for the rising generation while at the same time recording 'what History shows'.

5 *Conclusions*

I Three Forms of Bias

It seems that history textbooks for schools are affected by three sorts of bias. Firstly they are shaped by contemporary ideas on the nature of history, which at the turn of the century was seen as a structure and Britain as the master builder; from this secure position authors were able to pass strong moral judgements on the course of events. Between the Wars the building metaphor slides into an evolutionary one of 'natural growth' and there are less overt judgements on men as agents; nevertheless no author doubted that British history is like the growth of good seed which, in propitious conditions, could be transplanted, perhaps to Europe, but certainly to the Empire and Commonwealth. Today, since man can be characterised as neither a builder nor a gardener, history is told as an inevitable movement towards One World and doubts about the relevance of the story of nationalism seem to be resolved by writing history in either a detached or an 'objective' manner.

Secondly, there is the pressure of public examinations in which the criteria of hard fact and memorability prevail; to serve these demands, history is recounted in abridged and finite ways to provide model answers. Over 50 years ago, M. W. Keatinge suggested that documents should in part replace the clichés used as examination questions. These and supportive ideas have only recently taken root but orthodox examination methods have not been extirpated. As currently conceived much history-for-examinations leave the pupil, the teacher and the textbook in bondage to the facts and these are elevated into the ends of historical education.

The third form of bias—less commonly taken account of—is that arising from the personal response of the author to his world, his material and his task. Official and semi-official comments on textbooks often fail to find this of any significance at all; for example, W. H. Burston maintained that, '. . . the historian of the past writes in some detachment from the scene which he is portraying'[110] and 'One source of bias can surely be ruled out; personal self interest can hardly be affected by what we write about the past'.[111] It is hoped that this chapter has shown both these propositions to be untenable—at any rate for the authors of textbooks. For if these textbooks have anything in common (apart from a period of examinable history) it is that each author weaves into the text those values he wishes to impress upon 'varieties' of children— even to the extent of moralising over persons and events of which he can, due to existing historical ignorance, have scant knowledge. 'Omanesque' judgements provide the connecting link between authors whose works span some sixty years.

What purpose is served by holding an attitude—or more

[110] Ed. W. H. Burston and D. Thompson, *Studies in the Nature and Teaching of History* (Routledge, 1967, pp. 108-9).
[111] Ibid., p. 113.

accurately being held by an attitude about 'extravagance', 'disorder', 'idleness', 'charity' or any other concept is a question to which one might offer historical and psychological explanations. If contemporary authors seem less overtly biased than earlier writers, it may be that their attitudes serve different purposes or are more sophisticated or self-conscious; yet our views can still be nourished by slogans such as 'the inevitability of one world' or 'the Commonwealth is not an organisation but an idea'.

But this is not to suggest that history writing for schools and for current examination purposes could be different or that a text could not or should not be illuminated by the author's own values, but rather that to discount these forms of bias is to accept the illusion that textbooks are solely studies of the past.

II Is History about Storing or Processing?

If the study of history has a 'use', possibly it is that it discourages either complete rejection of the past or total allegiance to the present. To have criticised textbooks is to have looked at the needs they met; to welcome their dethronement is not necessarily to extol their successors—the aids which seem to have acquired their authority.

History textbooks belonged in a Victorian-Edwardian educational situation; this included the storehouse notions of faculty psychology, the examinability of knowledge, a short and work-orientated school life—with, in Fitch's words, 'textbooks as task-books', large classes and mainly unqualified teachers, meagre resources and a climate of opinion suspicious if not hostile to non-useful education. Today all these principles and practices are questioned; newer learning theories are united in their stress on 'experience' not storage as an aim of education; there are new modes of assessment; a longer and more liberally conceived school life; there are either smaller classes or more fluid groupings for children, staff and subjects (i.e., tutorial groups, team-teaching and 'integrated' studies); and what is done *with* a subject rather than what is the content *of* a subject often takes priority in curriculum planning; further, there is greater expenditure on and public concern over education. In this new situation a prolific array of teaching aids such as archive kits, pamphlets, project-kits and audio-visual material is seen, if not as expendable, at least as having a fairly limited life. And so, it might be asked, who could regret the passing of the history textbook any more than one could bemoan the scarcity of Edwardian boot button-hooks?

But even so, can the current trends be accepted wholeheartedly?

Earlier it was suggested that upon how it was believed children learn will rest much methodology. With the rapid and pervasive growth of social and developmental psychology there has come a good deal of agreement that 'experiencing' is the very stuff of education. The mind, once a storehouse to be stocked, may now be likened to a processing contrivance which can be energised by cavalcades of experiences; and it is believed that the quality and appropriateness of these experiences is important. Since today the area of childhood has been demarcated and children are recognised by their characteristic ways of thinking, feeling and doing, learning theorists and teachers are concerned with what they see as appropriate to age and stage; and whether according to Rousseau's fantasy or the experimental continuum of Dewey or in structured Piagetian stages, notions like discovery, exploration, activity, and creativity are, in effect, ways of labelling different sorts of experiences. The purpose of these experiences is enrichment. Jerome Bruner, referring to books, films, television, sound recordings and the like says, 'It does not serve much to dismiss such material as "merely for enrichment" since it is obvious that such enrichment is one of the principal objectives of education. Let us call these DEVICES FOR VICARIOUS EXPERIENCES'.[112]

Now whereas it is quite easy to criticise the old storehouse metaphor (and strangely, in the study of education what is out of fashion is often seen as faintly ridiculous or disgraceful), it may be difficult to see the implications of contemporary explanations of learning. For example, it is pertinent to ask if history ought to be seen as a mode of enquiry by which children are led to 'discover' their own answers, be 'constructionists' and 'generators' of new ideas? However admirable these objectives may be, if the study of history is to be *for* the sake of these activities rather than *by* means of these activities, then this would represent a pretty resounding defeat for those who claim that the state of HISTORICAL studies in schools is more enlightened than it was a hundred years ago; and if the cramming of abridged answers is to be replaced by 'experimental cavalcades' as the object of history teaching, then well might Whitehead's famous lines be depressingly appropriate— 'Every intellectual revolution which has ever stirred man into greatness has been a passionate protest against inert ideas. Then also with pathetic ignorance of human psychology it has proceeded by some educational scheme to bind humanity afresh with inert ideas of its own fashioning'.

[112] Jerome Bruner, *The Process of Education* (Harvard U.P., 1960, p. 81).

Peter Mitchell   *Humanities Programme*

THE decision to introduce into Thomas Bennett School a humanities programme, for all children, was the result of our dissatisfaction with a number of details involved in working the existing system. In the first place children were being asked to make choices, at the end of their third year, which resulted in some children discontinuing history and geography at a time when studies in these disciplines should be assuming a more analytical framework. Furthermore, the criteria for making these choices were often selected in the most arbitrary fashion: personalities of teachers often were more important than the educational value of the subject, in helping children to make their decisions. For the majority of children this situation therefore meant that, at the age of 14, they had completed their study of historical and contemporary events without savouring the opportunities for discussion and analysis, for which by interest and intellectual development they were becoming prepared.

Since September 1969, all children at Thomas Bennett have studied history continuously from their entry into the school until public examinations at the end of their fifth year. In the first three years history is taught as a separate discipline, for two periods per week, while in years 4 and 5 it forms part of a humanities programme, alongside geography and the social sciences, occupying eight periods per week. The organisation of a humanities programme resulted from the establishment of six faculties, in Easter 1967, representative of the academic life in the school. The English, Mathematics, Modern Languages, Science, Liberal Arts, and Humanities faculties each have their own head of faculty with department heads representing the constituent departments subsumed by each faculty. The main aims of this faculty organisation are to facilitate improved communication between the headmaster and the departments contained within faculties and to explore possible areas of curriculum development within faculties.

The constituent departments of the humanities faculty are: history, geography, social science (economics, sociology, psychology, law), religious education, the home economics and classics departments. Before establishing a humanities programme history became part of an option system at the end of Year 3 alongside geography, commerce and accounts. Out of a total of 400 pupils in the third year approximately 260 children were able to make the choice whether or not to continue studying history up to 'O' or C.S.E. level and an average of 140 annually made the choice in favour of history. Out of the 400 third-year pupils, 140 lower-ability children were excluded from making this choice and the humanities faculty provided for these an integrated studies programme, similar in outline to those referred to in the Schools Council Working Paper, 11. Historians contributed ideas, materials and teachers to the working of the integrated studies and worked in a 'team teaching' situation alongside geographers and social scientists.

* * *

This is the position usually adopted by the humanities in the curriculum. The humanities programme, first introduced in September 1969, radically changed this situation and introduced all children to thematic studies in their fourth and fifth years while continuing with separate history and geography in the first three years.

Our concern about existing examinations at 'O' level centred mainly on the amount of factual content demanded by both geography and history examinations. The breadth of work to be covered often leads to an emphasis on the accumulation of factual material and to uncritical thinking. In the quest for impressive results, staff are often forced into excessive use of 'chalk and talk' and children are consuming the ideas and opinions of the specialists without questioning the validity of their conclusions. If we wanted all children to continue studying history during their fourth and fifth years we had a responsibility to examine the content and modes of learning provided during these two years.

Our next two reasons for wishing to innovate are related most clearly to the problem of providing courses specifically in a comprehensive school. We saw that lower-ability children, numbering 160 out of a fourth year of 420 pupils, had been provided with an integrated studies course, run by the humanities faculty, which was inspired by the Schools Council Working Paper, 11, *Humanities and the Young School Leaver*. As originally planned the course rested heavily on the support of the local community organisations and contained little indication of how 14- and 15-year-old children

K

could have their horizons and thinking broadened. The course was modified somewhat to allow the introduction of social science (sociology and anthropology to be specific) into the curriculum, but it remained an uneasy compromise between the desire to teach the intellectual qualities of history and social science and the need to meet what were considered the special needs of lower-ability children to be introduced to their community. Above all the faculty objected to the explicit definition of a course designed for a particular group of children, many of whom resented the implications of not being allowed to make the choices open to their higher-ability contemporaries. As a faculty we saw our main responsibility as teaching the rational judgement of history and the social sciences (including geography). The degree to which this rationality can be taught to children of different abilities will depend upon the level to which they are able to work with concepts and analytical questions, and the quality of the modes of learning designed to take children through the validation process. As Professor Hirst has written: 'To deny the teaching of this rationality to some children, either because it is thought too difficult for them, or is for some reason less important for them, is to deny them the opportunity for rational development which is at the heart of the education process'.[113] A case is not being made to exclude all consideration of those elements of practical living, which are often central to integrated studies for lower-ability children, but for the clear distinction to be drawn between information about practical living and the rational development gained through work in history and the social sciences. The humanities programme aims to be a unifying element in the curriculum taught to children of all abilities.

At a similar level of argument we were concerned with 'O' level and C.S.E. examinations. The distinction between the two examinations can be so great that a choice has to be made between the two at the end of Year 3. For the large number of border-line candidates we wanted to delay this choice until the January of Year 5, and this meant similar basic areas of study in both examinations and similar methods of examining. The method of examining which we wished to follow, involved consideration of course work and necessitated the introduction of Mode 3 examinations for both 'O' and C.S.E. levels. In this way we were meeting our teaching needs, in terms of examinations, and at the same time the two public examinations were not dividing the border-line children into two defined groups at the end of their third year. It must be emphasised

[113] P. Hirst, 'The Logic of the Curriculum', *Journal of Curriculum Studies*, vol. no. 2, May 1969.

that in terms of achievement by children of different abilities these arguments for non-divisive courses and non-divisive examinations do not mean a move towards a mean level of achievement set by children of average ability. There is no point at which one can honestly divide the children into those suited to one particular type of course and examination and those to another.

Our final reason for introducing the humanities programme arose out of our wish to introduce a stronger social science content and possible expansion of argument into the curriculum. Sociology, anthropology, psychology and economics would allow aspects of contemporary society, which are often of immediate interest to children, to be studied. Drawing these disciplines into the programme, alongside history, avoided increasing the problem of choices placed as options to children at the end of Year 3. The claims made by social scientists for a place in the curriculum are often met at the expense of already established disciplines from the humanities. By drawing together staff representing these disciplines and creating a combined programme we hoped to develop more realistic choices for children within the programme rather than by setting one discipline against another.

Some experience in working as a team of teachers had been gained in running the integrated studies for lower-ability children. This course had been planned and some materials developed in one term from April to July 1967, and it was clear to all involved that this time was completely inadequate. The team of teachers responsible were often operating in areas outside their own disciplines and involved in inexpertly selecting and editing materials from the social sciences. Coupled with this, material was typed and reproduced by staff already heavily involved in their teaching of C.S.E., 'O' and 'A' levels in their respective disciplines. No books adequately met the needs of this course and if curriculum development was to be expanded to embrace the work of all children, in the fourth and fifth years, we had to spend a minimum of one year in defining objectives, content of syllabus, modes of learning and producing materials.

The school year 1968/69 was used as the planning year and in September we began the first of the Monday evening meetings, which involved all members of the department. At this stage an attempt was being made to stimulate a fresh evaluation of the logic of integration in a programme involving history and social science. We had first to be aware of the structure of the disciplines involved. The structure of a discipline may be divided into two parts. The first part consists of the concepts which define the subject matter and control its inquiries and the second part is its method of inquiry or proof process.

We also had to discuss the unique qualities of the disciplines that might make special contributions to the programme. Historians and geographers often use the concepts and at times the laws of the social sciences but to be more explicit in our treatment of sociology, economics, etc., as disciplines is to create an entirely new situation. Staff were now being asked to consider social science being taught alongside history in a single programme of work. Our discussions, when centring on such academic questions, may seem remote from the reality of work in the classroom but as a team of teachers concerned with specific disciplines we felt it essential to specify areas of possible incompatibility at as high a level of academic awareness as the discussions allowed. (The planning of integrated courses for lower-ability children are free from such academic debates largely because the children are unlikely to be candidates for advanced level study.) The history and geography departments were each represented by five members of staff, specialists in their respective disciplines who were rightly determined to see that their work was not subjected to a complete 'take-over' by the social sciences. With no clearly defined conceptual framework or validation process the historians felt that the questions they asked might be subsumed by the questions asked in more clearly defined disciplines, namely sociology and economics. Furthermore association with the social sciences might have reduced historians to providing background information to contemporary studies or might have elevated contemporary history to the exclusion of earlier periods. On this question of methodology there is undeniably a trend amongst certain historians to embrace the methods of the social sciences but the history department stressed that these analytical distinctions and 'model building' activities, which form the basis of social science methodology, are by their very nature exclusive of particulars and hence may be marginally, rather than centrally, appropriate to historical studies. Our discussions made it clear that the programme should pay due regard to the literary and artistic qualities of historical studies and strike a balanced use of social science methodology. The use of statistical methods is most appropriate in economic history and demography but to seek to apply them more broadly should be tempered with caution. 'Literary guidance and unsystematic data' are still necessary to illuminate the human experience which is at the heart of all history, including economic history.[114]

[114] Asa Briggs, 'Second Beginning', *Encounter*, Oct. 1969.

When we discussed the characteristics of disciplines in the humanities programme we were of course led to discuss objectives. Because we were involved in major curriculum change we needed to think precisely about our objectives, for they controlled the modes of learning, the evaluation and the content of the course. (In existing examinations, objectives are most often left implicit and are only discovered by studying syllabuses and examiners' reports over a number of years.) Our concern with the distinctions to be drawn between the social sciences and history made us concerned about cognitive objectives and about developing a mode of inquiry appropriate to these studies. Fenton's *Guide to the New Social Studies* outlines, in the chapter on objectives and evaluation, a method of inquiry which organises the hypotheses formation and the proof process parts of a method of inquiry into sequential and coherent steps.

1. Recognition of a problem from data.
2. Formulating a hypothesis:
   (a) Asking analytical questions;
   (b) Stating hypotheses.
3. Gathering data:
   (a) Deciding what data will be needed;
   (b) Selecting or rejecting sources.
4. Analysing, examining and interpreting data:
   (a) Selecting relevant data;
   (b) Evaluating sources to determine the author's frame of reference;
   (c) Interpreting data.
5. Evaluating the hypotheses in light of the data.

Our main concern is not with imparting a prescribed factual content but with teaching children a mode of inquiry. The qualities of critical thought often demanded by history teachers and lecturers, impatient with the existing demands of 'O' level history, involve the ability to relate cause and effect; the detection of bias; inference from data and evaluation of evidence; the ability to select and use material relevantly, all of which are part of, or legitimate modifications of, Fenton's 'Mode of Inquiry'. Learning to operate a mode of inquiry is at the heart of developing the rational judgement associated with history and the social sciences.

Objectives in the affective domain have understandably proved more difficult to define. This is partly because the basic changes in attitude, which result from following such a programme, may not manifest themselves until long after the children have left school.

There is also the danger of oversimplifying the situation by appearing to see affective and cognitive objectives as always distinctive. One of our principal concerns in teaching a mode of inquiry must be the development of a certain attitude towards evidence that causes the two domains to merge at the onset of studies. In the treatment of factual evidence and moral questions a humanities programme must have a responsibility for helping children to see the autonomous nature of decisions involving fundamental areas of human values and beliefs; the uncertainty arises when attempting to specify the changes in behaviour that result from making these studies. Historians have traditionally made claims for the importance of historical studies in helping children develop moral judgement and indeed one of the major contributions of history must be in its insistence on the autonomy of historical investigation. Our emphasis on cognitive objectives does not signify neglect of the affective area in our teaching, but rather a determination to make explicit statements about objectives in the average intellectual development, where evaluation is possible, rather than in the emotional (affective) area where we remain sceptical about testing the outcome of our teaching.

The selections of content for inclusion in the course reflects the balanced interplay of ideas from the constituent departments. We considered the age of the children and their interests; we made a prognosis of concepts likely to be important after leaving school and finally we considered the balance of disciplines involved in the course. In emphasising the structures of disciplines we have predetermined that the content should be a vehicle for the teaching of the concepts central to the structures of history and the social sciences. We had no wish to pursue interdisciplinary work for its own sake and we also had no wish to use a formula that determined the proportion of a theme to be devoted to a particular discipline. The idea of disciplines working together was to grow naturally out of the study of the themes chosen. Bearing these points in mind, the themes chosen for study have in a sense predictably included those broad areas of human concern defined by Laurence Stenhouse for inclusion in the School's Council *Humanities Project. War, The Family, Education, The Underdeveloped World, Land Use and Urban Studies, Post-1850 Demographic Studies, The General Strike and the Depression, Post-1850 Growth of Industry, and Agricultural Change, International Relations*, are examples of themes covered in the two-year programme. Of these *The Underdeveloped World* furnishes an example of a theme which benefits from an interdisciplinary approach with geographical emphasis being focused on physical

environment, economics drawing out the problems facing aid programmes, and anthropology focusing on the problem of cultural
change brought about by changing technology. On the other hand,
The General Strike and the Depression involves a detailed patch study
of a theme which in its treatment is most accurately described as an
historical study. A common factor in all themes is relevance, in
that we have attempted to draw together themes that will help
children to comprehend some of the realities of the modern world.
Making judgements about events taking place a century ago is
heightened by the pupils' improved understanding of contemporary
society and by drawing on the pupils' direct experience of the type
of events under study.

Without preliminary planning, integration may well create an
environment in which neither staff nor pupils have a sense of place,
time or purpose. This point becomes particularly clear when it is
fully appreciated that the underlying pedagogic theory under integration is likely to be self-regulatory. Teaching a *mode of inquiry* of
necessity implies, as far as both the history and social science contents are concerned, that the pupils will have opportunities to work
as historians and social scientists, handling the raw materials of
studies in these disciplines. Successful inquiry involving critical
thought is likely to change the teacher-pupil-authority relationship,
in particular to increasing the status of the pupil in the learning
situation. Interpersonal relationships between teacher and pupil
will be closer and a harmony established between the social and
academic relationships in the school. Furthermore, a genuinely
personal encounter of teacher and pupil may be one of the most
important means through which many children in a pluralistic
society can develop some capacity to make considered, autonomous,
moral judgements.

Bernstein[115] has suggested that we might be currently witnessing a
change away from 'closed' schools, in which a specific set of values
is transmitted through rituals which enable the individual to
develop a clear sense of identity (even if defined in reaction *against*
the ritualised values), towards 'open' schools in which there is only
consensus at the level of very general values and in which identity
may become problematic. In such schools, Bernstein argues, the
transmission of values (and the capacity to think seriously about
moral issues) will rest very largely at the interpersonal level. His
fear is that university selection pressures will force the 'open' school
to treat its pupils bureaucratically, thus inhibiting the development

[115] In 'Ritual in Education', *Philosophical Transactions of the Royal Society of London*,
No. 772.

of genuinely personal relations between pupils and teachers and thus encouraging pupils to turn to the informal peer group as a major source of values, relationship and identity. In a New Town like Crawley the reality of this latter situation is more significant than in older-established communities because the basic family unit is the nuclear family and close ties with adult numbers of the extended family are not characteristic of a child's experience. This relationship with adults outside one's immediate nuclear family may be seen increasingly as the school's responsibility. The self-regulated learning, that is an essential part of curriculum development under discussion, is in part an attempt to stabilise the pattern of relationships experienced by the child in the school.

The use of documents and other original source material is basic to the innovation of the programme. But gathering together the materials and reproducing them presented a major problem. The quality of reproduction had proved fundamental to the success of materials in the integrated studies course for lower ability children and the faculty was fortunate to receive a grant from the Centre for Educational Technology at Sussex University for the planning year 1968/69. The grant was used to pay for one extra full-time member of staff for the year, and secretarial support for two and a half days per week. This has enabled us to produce flexible kits of materials for each of the themes being taught, although much of the work on the kits had still to be undertaken after the planning year ended. Secretarial support has since been forthcoming from West Sussex Education Committee.

Our main sources for original historical documents have been the Record Offices of West and East Sussex County Councils and the British Museum Newspaper Library at Colindale. The photostats of these documents are covered with a protective plastic cover and displayed in the humanities area, so that children can study the originals if necessary. The typed copies of documents are reproduced on white foolscap paper, for use in the classroom. A complete kit will normally consist of:

(a) Written documents together with individual document work cards designed to suggest to staff and/or children how the document can be used.

(b) Statistical evidence reproduced on yellow foolscap sheets.

(c) Slides either made from film strips or taken with the faculties' 35 mm reflex camera.

(d) Multiple copies of black and white photographs. These are usually originally photographed with the reflex camera and then mounted before a plate is made of them and multiple copies reproduced by the West Sussex County Council's offset printing machines.

(e) Tape recordings either of original historical recordings or of staff reading literary or other documentary evidence.

A complete list of all materials available in a kit is printed for staff together with an indication of the ability range that might successfully use the materials. The staff responsible for producing kits also produce a narrative outline of the problem or patch to be studied. This is kept by students in their folders to act as a guide when planning their inquiries.

A kit is designed to be flexible allowing staff to organise a variety of modes of learning. Two weeks of self-regulated inquiry may be preceded by a descriptive introduction to the theme designed to stimulate pupils' interest; because staff work as a team, planning and producing materials, these introductory lessons often take the form of two or three classes coming together while one member of staff presents a carefully prepared introduction usually making use of a variety of teaching aids. The increased importance of self-regulated learning does not place less value on the teacher's ability to engage a class interest in a particular aspect of their studies. It should however help to give a more precise distinction to the type of content pupils should discuss, independently inquire into, or be told about.

Geographers have traditionally been provided with specialist rooms but historians are normally less fortunate. Establishing a humanities programme made it necessary to create an area of rooms that would allow the pupils' work to take maximum advantage of the materials being developed. This was partially achieved by moving the geography department to the top floor giving four adjacent teaching rooms, two stores, an office and space for the creation of a resource centre. Considerable improvisation, undertaken by members of the department, was needed to make this area moderately suitable for the immediate needs of the programme when teaching first began in September 1969. Shelving was erected, two doorways created to provide access between rooms and two partitions constructed. The school is currently undergoing a building programme which includes internal reorganisation of rooms in the lower and upper schools. This will provide unified humanities areas in both schools which in the upper school, where the programme will be taught, includes provision of seven classrooms, each with basic overhead projector, screens and storage units, a projects and lecture room capable of seating eighty children and a central resource centre.

The working environment is often considered of little importance in secondary schools in contrast with the best primary schools. The movement of children between departments prevents children from feeling an affinity with any one environment. Successful inquiry rests, however, upon children moving with confidence to collect and organise their materials and efficient material storage is needed at the centre of any working area. The area must be instinctively associated with learning in the humanities.

The resource centre we have developed in the present humanities area embodies many of the organising principles we plan to include in the new resource centre. The system that we used was selected because it is capable of handling a variety of materials and because it can be used equally well by all the disciplines represented in the programme. As each piece of material is collected for inclusion in the centre it is analysed and the concepts covered in the material are noted. For example an 1876 government report on factories might cover the concepts of working conditions, child labour, legislation. If the piece of material is the 100th collected the accession number 100 is then noted on the concept cards, one of which is available for each concept covered by the collection. Because the material collected includes historical documents we have also inserted time cards covering 25-year periods so that the document referred to being dated 1870 would also have its accession number 100 noted on the time card 1850-75. Working in reverse if one wished to extract a piece of material on the effect of technological changes on the location of the steel industry in the second half of the nineteenth century one would extract the concept cards, technology, invention, industrial location, steel industry, and the time cards 1850-75 and 1875-1900. The accession numbers common to all six cards would indicate which materials covered this subject. For items other than printed documents a prefix is used in order to indicate whether the item is, for example, a film of tapes and such exceptional pieces may be numbered in the same series as the printed materials though stored separately. Maintaining the resource centre with a constant input of relevant current newspaper articles, magazine articles and historical documents has developed into such a time-consuming exercise that there is little doubt the faculty requires ancillary help in much the same way as laboratory technicians operate in the science faculty.

The importance of an organised teaching environment has been reaffirmed in the first year's teaching of the course. Half the teaching time for all groups has to be spent in huts outside the humanities area. This prevents children from using a resource area and makes it necessary for staff to carry documents into the classroom, which in a sense controls the range of inquiry possible. Couple this with the fact that the huts are in no sense humanities rooms and the contrast in child motivation between the humanities area and the huts, while disturbing to staff, has been entirely predictable. Until the full humanities area is completed the highest hopes of the programme will not be achieved. We have also faced particular language problems in the use of documents with lower ability children. Our approach has too frequently emphasised the use of technical language (concepts) appropriate to particular disciplines, notably the social sciences, when the use of 'common sense' language and the explicit relating of the introduction themes to the pupil's own experiences would frequently offer a more meaningful start to a topic. Producing a course which embraces children of all abilities has in its first year, despite its avowed objectives, met the particular interests and abilities of 'O' level pupils more precisely than C.S.E. level and non-exam candidates. Willingness to accept a course designed around the concepts and methodologies of disciplines fits most clearly into the expectations and interests of the 'O' level pupils. An immediate problem we therefore face is whether documents presented to lower-ability pupils should be put in a language which they can understand, while attempting to retain the ideas and perspectives represented in the documents. Alternatively, or in addition, we need to broaden the range of ways in which documents are used in the classroom. A kit is designed to be flexible, but by designing work cards for each document the pupils' experience of using documents has often been repetitive. This is also accounted for by the newness and quantity of materials produced which have presented staff with the problem of thoroughly mastering their contents. It is true to say that staff have sometimes taken refuge in the materials, presenting them in the simplest and often most unimaginative fashion.

Our first-year experiences have also emphasised the need for a more flexible timing of themes; genuine inquiry that has stimulated a pupil's interest may be curtailed by a rigidly timed programme of thematic studies. The main problem here is the use of key lessons and films which have to be planned, and thus timed, in advance. One of our first moves will be to make available the materials for two themes simultaneously and provide individual staff with greater freedom to assess the appropriate time for themes to change.

On the positive side, the first year has produced encouraging results where inquiry has proceeded from a guided start to a more open-ended project in which pupils have gathered information to use as evidence alongside that provided by the kits. Many pupils have become particularly proficient at collecting newspaper and magazine articles on economic, political and social events and knitting them into their inquiries by commenting on their content and discussing its relevance to the issue they are studying. They are encouraged to see the value of relevant articles from any of the weekly newspapers so that the 'quality' press is not providing a minority of pupils with exclusive evidence for their inquiries. The narratives developed have shown a gathering confidence in handling evidence and their ideas contained therein, and a realisation of what it means to develop a personal understanding of a problem through study in depth. For those children less proficient at expressing themselves in written narratives it may be necessary to judge the development of their responses to evidence mainly through the medium of recorded discussions. At present, course work needs careful consideration before we can seriously contemplate the inclusion of taped material.

An innovation involving the introduction of a programme of work for all children in their fourth and fifth year should be the subject of careful evaluation. Reports of progress in educational innovation are all too frequently over-optimistic; the mere fact that we are involved in innovation within a large comprehensive school of over 2,000 pupils is sufficient to convince many observers that this is a progressive development, superior in all ways to what is being replaced. If we are to help children to take a critical attitude towards evidence, or as the historian might say to 'suspect anything that is new', then it is incumbent on us as teachers to take this aspect of our work seriously.

The direct link between objectives and evaluation should be clear; without being precise about what we are trying to achieve it is impossible to construct any meaningful test items. We intend to test knowledge of *content* partly on the basis of objective tests. A pupil's mastery over elements of the *mode of inquiry* may also be measured partly through objective testing, for example selecting the most appropriate analytical questions to test a given hypothesis. The main test, however, will require pupils to demonstrate their ability to carry on independent investigation and the emphasis on course work as the basis for 50 per cent of the final grades awarded at 'O' and C.S.E. levels will allow us to evaluate independent work undertaken over a period of time greater than that available for normal written exams. The written exam will include work on documents as well as essay and objective questions. Three grades at 'O' and C.S.E. will be awarded in history, geography and social science. It will be possible for pupils to gain a combination of 'O' and C.S.E. grades according to the quality of their work, and some pupils may receive only one grade at C.S.E.

If children are to be given the opportunity to consider, in an informed manner, the major political, social and economic events both in the contemporary historical and current affairs contexts, then the arbitrariness of curriculum options and the emphasis on teaching an agreed corpus of knowledge, in the majority of 'O' level history and geography syllabuses, must both be brought into question. The integrated solution described here is one possible solution to the need for children to be taught the tools of inquiry methods. The pressure on the curriculum is increasing; teachers of politics are rightly asking that children be given the opportunity to study British politics. Professor Bernard Crick's chapter on the introducing of politics into schools[116] makes the case for a more realistic approach to the teaching of politics which would involve a move away from the traditional approach through British Constitution to the central consideration of the *ideas* and *action* that make up politics. Professor Asa Briggs in reviewing *Men and Societies*, edited by Robert Smith, which includes experimental courses in the humanities and social sciences, commented on the obvious lack of consideration for economics in the courses. Economics, like politics, can be exciting; when approached as part of the fabric of everyday life its relevance has an appeal to children of all abilities.

[116] In *The Teaching of Politics*, edited by D. B. Heater (Methuen, 1969), especially pp. 14, 16.

4

HOW FAR BEYOND
BEGINNINGS?

William Lamont

In the Privy Purse accounts of the Marquis of Hertford in 1641/2 the following item is recorded: 'Paid for a history book and a cane for my Lord Beauchamp, fourteene shillings.'[1] Why do the history book and the cane go so well together? They ought not to do so. Presumably most teachers of history want to communicate to their pupils something of the romance that the past evoked for them, want to instil in their pupils a sense of curiosity about their ancestors. This was as true of history teachers in Victorian times as in our own day. The Assistant Masters' Association booklet, *The Teaching of History in Secondary Schools*, reproduces pages from two best-selling Victorian history textbooks: Ince's *Outlines of English History*, and Mangnall's *Historical Questions*. Both are appallingly dreary. Ince contains great slabs of information which he expected the children to commit to memory. Mangnall consists of a breathless series of questions and answers—'When did Milton live? In Cromwell's time to whom he was Latin Secretary. . . . Why did Richard Cromwell resign the protectorship? Because he did not possess those great qualities which were necessary to support the views of his father, Oliver Cromwell,' and so on. We might add one more: 'What were the names of the two history textbooks which made history so joyless for Victorian children? Ince and Mangnall were those textbooks.'

But if that was their effect, that was not their intention. That is why there is pathos in reading Ince's preface:

> 'Do the actions of our *own* ancestors present nothing to arrest the attention, or captivate the heart? Peruse the historic page; the magnanimity of a Russell, the achievements of a Marlborough, the daring of a Nelson, must give the answer. Happily, then, the fault is not the dryness of our annals, but rather in the defects of the books written professedly for the use of schools.'

And equally in Mangnall's apology for her questions:

> 'They are intended to awaken a spirit of laudable curiosity in young minds.'[2]

What went wrong? Why did they produce books which seemed calculated only to *deaden* a spirit of curiosity; to make it *impossible* for young children to identify with the magnanimity of a Russell, the achievements of a Marlborough, the daring of a Nelson?

These questions are equally relevant today. Martin Booth recently asked a group of history teachers to define their aims. The results were unsurprising:

> 'Mr Black listed the following aims:
> 1. To teach children to think and to doubt both the textbook and myself.
> 2. To sympathise and understand—different problems, different people, different attitudes.
> 3. To begin to put our own society into some kind of historical perspective.
> 4. To have banished some ignorance.
>
> It seems clear that he is concerned with emotional as well as mental goals, and that he sees history learning as something which involves the whole personality. These aims are held by all the teachers and phrases such as 'development of interest and enjoyment' (Miss Denton), 'taking notice of the history around them' (Mr Freeman), or 'an appreciation and understanding of other men's ideas and achievements' (Miss Spender), would be accepted by them all—partly because of their high level of generality.'

But Booth's investigations did not stop there. He asked the pupils of these same history teachers to describe how their history lessons appeared to *them*:

> 'An analysis of the answers to question 13 shows that most pupils consider history lessons to consist of learning facts, reading textbooks, listening to the class teacher, note-making and taking dictated notes.'[3]

As Booth properly reminds us, we ought not to take too seriously the uninformed criticisms of the pupils. But the greater danger lies in the opposite direction: of not taking their criticisms seriously enough. There is a menacing credibility gap at present when the claims for our subject advance, as the interest of the pupils themselves recedes. Mary Price has recently pointed out that history came bottom of the poll for interest and enjoyment in a survey of 9,677 early school leavers.[4]

The failures of Ince and 'Mr Black' may be related ones. We get a clue in a significant aside, on a later occasion, which 'Mr Black' makes to Booth:

> 'Certain topics select themselves against your better judgement. For example . . . in the second year, I think somewhere, somehow, the Reformation has to come in, if only superficially, because otherwise this will never be done and they'll never hear of Old Luther and that sort of thing . . .'[5]

We kill by conscientiousness. We feel an obligation to impart information from the highest of motives: we feel that we have failed our children somehow if they haven't heard of 'Old Luther and that sort of thing'. We feel that we can reconcile this aim with our other aims—involving our children with figures from the past and instilling in them a sense of curiosity and romance—and are not sufficiently honest in acknowledging to ourselves how often, in pursuing one goal, we subvert the other.

'Mr Black' seems to be, in this, more culpable than Ince. However much Ince may have wanted his young readers to re-create the 'magnanimity of a Russell' he knew that this was subsidiary to his highest duty: to transmit to them that body of information which made up history. The philosophy of history which Ince outlined in his preface to the *Outlines of English History* was one that was perfectly acceptable, not only to his fellow-teachers, but to the professional historians who trained them at the universities:

> 'The importance of having the outlines of every study accurately defined, and the leading points and bearings correctly acquired before the *minutiae* are entered into, will be readily conceded; and also that if the groundwork be clearly traced in early life, it will scarcely ever be obliterated; but that subsequent reading, and even conversation, will continue to supply materials for the completion of the sketch.'

Contrast his position with that of 'Mr Black' who, when pressed by Booth on the necessity for his pupils to know about Luther, shamefacedly conceded that 'this is perhaps a guilt complex we shouldn't have'. We shouldn't have such a guilt complex because, in our understanding of the nature of history, we have moved such a distance from the assumptions which governed Ince and his colleagues. E. H. Carr, in the first chapter of his *What is History?*, has wittily summarised that revolution: at its heart is the recognition that the Victorians were wrong to abase themselves before the historical fact. Carr asserts:

> 'The facts are really not at all like fish on the fishmonger's slab. They are like fish swimming about in a vast and sometimes inaccessible ocean; and what the historian catches will depend, partly on chance, but mainly on what part of the ocean he chooses to fish in and what tackle he chooses to use —these two factors being, of course, determined by the kind of fish he wants to catch. By and large, the historian will get the kind of facts he wants. History means interpretation.'[6]

Carr isolates three weaknesses in the Victorians' reverence for facts. First, the facts of history never come to us 'pure': 'they are always refracted through the mind of the recorder'. Second, the historian needs 'imaginative understanding for the minds of the people with whom he is dealing, for the thought behind their acts'. Third, 'we can view the past, and achieve our understanding of the past, only through the eyes of the present'. If all this is true, its consequences for the teaching of our subject in the classroom are immense. The Victorians wanted to arouse the historical imagination of their pupils, but had to reconcile this with the obligation to lay a factual foundation for the subject: to trace a groundwork, as Ince said, that would subsequently be scarcely ever obliterated. We are freed from this constraint; we can say, with the authors of *The Teaching of History*, that the long-term consequences of what the history teacher does will 'not be the facts that linger, but the attitudes of mind that are formed'.

The most striking feature of history teaching in schools today, however, has been the continued sovereignty of the 'facts that linger'. 'Mr Black' acknowledges its irrationality, but cannot emancipate himself from a sense of guilt if he fails to cover the facts. As early as 1929, University historians were becoming alarmed at the extent to which their colleagues in the schools remained loyal to Ince; a conference at that date revealed the University teachers pleading for a 'training in critical method and a scholarly mental outlook' while the schoolteachers extolled 'the merits of imparting exact historical knowledge in more or less formidable doses'.[7] The textbooks that continued to be used in the classroom, and the examination papers that continued to be set, alike testified to the victory of Ince. The most significant departures from Ince's day— interest in contemporary history, in 'line of development' syllabuses, in Social Studies programmes—were pseudo-revolutions in that

L

they still upheld the merits of imparting exact historical knowledge in more or less formidable doses; only the nature of the doses
themselves changed with fashion. And so a radical of the 1930's
like M. V. C. Jeffreys could *boast* of his 'line of development' reformed syllabus:

> 'Dates must be learnt as before. But to the unprejudiced mind
> there is no reason why key dates in the development of trans-
> port, trade, exploration, art and science should not be as
> good a framework as lists of kings, battles, treaties and Acts
> of Parliament.'[8]

Or as bad a framework? It is time that we explored the failure of
school history to adapt to the changed way that historians themselves now feel about their subject.

Before we do that, we must establish that Carr is correct in
arguing that his colleagues *have* changed in the way that he described. In making this claim, Carr acknowledges his debt to 'the
Oxford philosopher and historian Collingwood, the only British
thinker in the present century who has made a serious contribution
to the philosophy of history'.[9] But Carr follows Collingwood only
part of the way: in the rejection of 'fact-worship'. Collingwood's
positive contribution, his emphasis on the role of the historical
imagination in 're-creating' past thought, carries with it equal
dangers. And Carr does think of them as *equally* false. He sees the
historian's task as steering delicately 'between the Scylla of an untenable theory of history as an objective compilation of facts' and
'the Charybdis of an equally untenable theory of history as the sub-
jective product of the mind of the historian'. Yet Carr's own navigation is not delicate enough for master-mariner G. R. Elton, who
smites him, on several pages in his *The Practice of History*, for his
'extreme relativism'.[10] The muddles of 'Mr Black' become more
intelligible in the light of these academic disputes: the school-
teacher—no longer as confident as his Victorian predecessor about
the merits of factual information but profoundly wary about the
historical imagination—is mirroring in this the unease of his professional colleagues.

Yet Professor Elton has himself warned in another context that,
because 'historians are so fond of parading their disagreements',
the real consensus among them may be overlooked.[11] Now the
impression that Carr gives is that Collingwood's 'imagination' is as
bogus as Ince's 'fact'. That impression is false, as we see when we
look closer at Carr's case against Collingwood. Carr says that 'the
emphasis on the role of the historian *tends, if pressed to its logical*

conclusion, to rule out any objective history at all: history is what the historian makes'. He goes on to say that 'Collingwood *seems* indeed *at one moment*, in an *unpublished* note quoted by his editor, to have reached this conclusion'. Again he accuses Collingwood of coming '*perilously near* to treating history as something spun out of the human brain'. He says that 'a still greater danger *lurks in* the Collingwood hypothesis' of maintaining that 'the criterion of a right interpretation is its suitability to some present purpose'. The italics are mine, not Carr's: they denote heavy qualifications that prevent us from saying that Collingwood *was* committed to those positions. Without the italics, in close juxtaposition, the whole passage conveys the impression that Collingwood believed that history *was* something spun out of the human brain: a few paragraphs on this becomes the 'Charybdis' which the historian must avoid.[12]

All this is brutally unfair to Collingwood, who went to some trouble to differentiate the task of the historian from that of the historical novelist: above all, in the fact that 'the historian's picture stands in a peculiar relation to something called evidence'.[13] There is not time here to undertake a full explanation of what Collingwood *did* say; but at least we can establish what he did *not* say. And 'a peculiar relation to' was not a euphemism for distortion or suppression or invention: it involved essentially that 'reciprocity' which Carr claimed as *his* middle way. Nor did Collingwood rule out 'objective' history. The concept is a difficult one, but Christopher Blake's essay on it clears up some misconceptions. To paraphrase crudely a complex argument,[14] we use 'objective' in a specialised, philosophical sense and in an ordinary, everyday sense as (almost) synonymous with 'integrity'. Collingwood rules out 'objectivity' in the first sense, it is true, but denies that we then have to slide into total scepticism and a rejection of 'objectivity' in the second sense. Collingwood's practice was consistent with his theory: he was a first-class professional historian. Elton has complained that the assault on facts in history has come from people 'who did not as a rule try to write history'. Grumpily, he concedes that this does not hold true of Collingwood, but less than handsomely adds:

> 'When, like R. G. Collingwood, they did, it is not possible to analyse their history in the terms of their philosophy: it is just ordinary sound history.'[15]

Carr and Elton have also written 'ordinary sound history'; and like Collingwood, they have also done it superlatively well. They have done it on principles remarkably similar to Collingwood's.

Collingwood warns that the historian, unlike the novelist, is in 'a peculiar relation to something called evidence'; Carr speaks of the 'reciprocity' between the historian and his facts; Elton speaks of 'imagination, controlled by learning and scholarship, learning and scholarship rendered meaningful by imagination'. The popular impression of Elton as an apologist for Victorian 'fact-worshippers' is totally erroneous. He dismisses them in a sentence: 'This naïve theory concerning the facts of history, possible once widely current, has suffered sufficient bludgeoning to require no discussion here.' Elton speaks of the importance of an 'ability to analyse problems, and to grasp larger wholes imaginatively', among the highest skills of an historian; indeed, he argues that 'it, rather than the acquiring of a body of knowledge, is the proper end of education, and that the study of history is exceptionally well qualified to teach it'. Finally, he affirms boldly that 'history is a subject . . . in which to teach cannot mean merely to convey information or instruct in techniques but must mean to assist in the formation of a given type of trained mind'.[16]

What perversity then makes Carr play down Collingwood's stress on the importance of evidence, makes Elton play down Carr's insistence on reciprocity? I would argue: not perversity, but scrupulousness. Once assume that the Victorian case for accumulating factual information has been defeated, a rival nightmare confronts the historian: the danger of relativism. Let the case for the historian using his imagination be put a shade too insensitively and an abyss opens before the historian. Here it is possible to feel not too sorry for Collingwood or Carr. Both loved the striking phrase; both delivered their thoughts on the historian's craft in the form originally of lectures. Phrases like 'the history of thought, and therefore all history, is the re-enactment of past thought in the historian's own mind' (Collingwood) or 'the historian will get the kind of facts he wants' (Carr) must have been difficult to resist making—although not, one would have thought, impossible. They obscured the common sense that underlay them; tragically for the teaching of history in the classroom, they obscured the very real agreement that now existed among professional historians.

And so Carr was driven to remind Collingwood of the dangers in 'the more extreme products of Soviet and anti-Soviet schools of historiography' even although one of Collingwood's most celebrated passages is his rejection of 'pigeon-holing' history, whether perpetrated by a Toynbee—or Marx[17]; and so Elton was driven to complain that Carr's 'relativism makes the historian the creator o history' even although Carr had pointed out that he had seen 'too many examples of extravagant interpretation riding roughshod over facts' not to be impressed with the dangers of relativism. Thus a teaching of history which does little more than *catalogue* facts is welcomed as at least an antidote to the type of history which *manipulates* facts. But, as Norman Mailer has pointed out, this is no cure:

> 'A neurotic may suffer agonies returning to his past; so may a nation which is not well. The neurotic recites endless lists of his activities and offers no reaction to any of it. So do we teach with empty content and by rigid manner where there is anxiety in the lore . . . we do not create a better nation by teaching school-children the catalogues of the White House.'[18]

Or catalogues of battles and treaties, Reform Bills and labour movements, we might add. This response, moreover, is as unnecessary as it is ineffective. In dethroning *facts*, we enthrone, not *opinion* or *dogma*, but *evidence*. Indeed, to Collingwood, the Victorian fact-worshipper and the Marxist 'pigeon-holer' were equally culpable in their uncritical approach to authorities. Ince's confidence in building up a solid edifice of history 'if the groundwork be clearly traced in early life' has its parallel in the faith of the young Marxist, Rubashov, in Arthur Koestler's novel, *Darkness at Noon*:

> 'History knows no scruples and no hesitation. Inert and unerring, she flows towards her goal. At every bend in her course she leaves the mud which she carries and the corpses of the drowned. History knows her way. She makes no mistakes. He who has not absolute faith in History does not belong in the Party's ranks.'

Now, to Collingwood, both Ince and Rubashov are regarding the historical fact in the way that an adolescent schoolboy regards the body of a woman: ignorance invests it with a magical quality. The biology teacher, who makes clear to the schoolboy the mechanics of human reproduction, is not thereby a rapist. Collingwood, in making clear the mechanics of how the historical 'fact' comes to us, of the contingent nature of historical evidence, is not thereby a relativist. Both destroy magic in order to induce not scorn, but understanding.

Nor, in stressing the importance of 'imagination', was Collingwood decrying the importance of evidence. This is clear in the analogy he borrowed from detective fiction. Half-jokingly, he suggested that the changed role of the detective in fiction reflected a wider change. In Victorian times, the model detective was Sherlock Holmes, 'the human bloodhound', who crawled about the floor collecting everything, no matter what, which might conceivably turn out to be a clue. Contrast him with a more recent detective hero, Agatha Christie's Monsieur Poirot, who despises such methods and insists on using 'the little grey cells'. Collingwood argues that by this he means that you cannot collect your evidence *before* you begin thinking, because thinking means asking questions, and nothing is evidence except in relation to some definite question. It does not mean that Poirot spins *solutions* out of his own mind; only *questions*. Sherlock Holmes had a brother, Mycroft, who *was* only an arm-chair theoriser. Collingwood might well have used him as a paradigm of the Victorian distrust of the imagination. For, although Mycroft was very clever, he was also inordinately lazy. He could never bestir himself out of his arm-chair. And, for all his ingenuity, this is the mark of his inferiority to Sherlock: *he lacked the patience to collect facts*. Under Carr's attack, Collingwood becomes a Mycroft-figure, when he is in reality a Poirot.

Does all this matter to the young teacher? Yes, because the effect of reading Elton and Carr is to leave him as mistrustful of the 'imagination' as of the 'fact'. Indeed, the 'imagination' can be seen merely as a holiday from the 'fact'. Thus, in F. J. C. Hearnshaw's deservedly yellowing book, *The 'Ifs' of History* (first published in 1929), the author speculates on various crises in history. What would have happened if Antony had not met Cleopatra? If Hannibal had not crossed the Alps? And so on. . . . In a foreword, he speaks feelingly of 'an opportunity such as is not often granted to an historian to let his imagination play around the hard facts with which he is familiar'.[19] It was Collingwood's great achievement to rescue the imagination from this trivial role, and to show that its true function was not ornamental, but structural.

The present *impasse* that history teaching has reached is this: we jeer only at the Victorians' reverence for facts, not at their contempt for the imagination. Somehow the 'historical imagination' still seems to connote dotty old ladies re-creating the Court of Versailles on an English lawn. We catalogue items for children to memorise, no longer with Ince's conviction in a storehouse of information, but—as Mailer perceptively observed—with a Cold War neurotic's terror of historical relativism. And so 'Mr Black', while knowing that he shouldn't, goes on having a guilt complex about leaving out 'Old Luther'. Had 'Mr Black' digested Collingwood properly, he would have been liberated from the tyranny of facts-that-must-be-known. For, although we have argued strongly that Collingwood was not a relativist—that is, in his *philosophy* of history—he *was* one, in the *content* of historical syllabuses. It did not matter what *content* you taught; it mattered terribly by what *method* you taught it. Collingwood felt sorry for an historian 'working against the grain of his own mind because it is demanded of him that he should study such uncongenial subjects, or because they are "in the period" which his own misguided conscience fancies he ought to treat in all its aspects'. And he warned of the consequences: he will 'merely repeat the statements that record the external facts of its development: names and dates, and ready-made descriptive phrases'.[20]

Most schemes for reforming the teaching of history in recent years have derived from almost the opposite position to that argued by Collingwood: it doesn't matter what *method* you teach, as long as you change the *content*. Constipated facts about Peel's Bank Charter Act, which children learned by rote, give way to constipated facts about what Professor Trevor-Roper has called the 'unrewarding gyrations of barbarous tribes in picturesque but irrelevant corners of the globe',[21] which children learn by rote; children stop copying down passages from textbooks as musty as Ince and start copying down passages from glossy Jackdaw-type archive kits; children learn Model Answers on the Origins of the Second World War instead of learning Model Answers on the Origins of the Crimean War.[22] Most notorious of all, schemes for integrating subjects have rested on the primacy of *content*: history has been used as a milch-cow for other disciplines, as in the ill-fated 'Social Studies' programmes of the 1950's. It is good, therefore, to see the recent Schools Council paper declare firmly that 'history's contribution to a humanities curriculum is not a body of facts and concepts';[23] it is good to see that Peter Mitchell welcomes our subject within his Humanities programme, not for its content, but for its *mode of inquiry*; it is good, finally, to see Sybil Marshall developing the historical skills of the most surprised group of headmasters who ever enrolled on a M.A. course upon no firmer groundwork, *pace* Ince, than a poem by Andrew Marvell![24]

The antithesis of *content* and *mode of inquiry* is, up to a point, a false one. No teaching of *content* in the past has ever excluded the possibility of the pupil's developing historical skills; no teaching a *mode of inquiry* can exist in a vacuum, and the skills developed will have to be exercised on an area of content. Still, the shift in priorities is fundamental. Edwin Fenton put it like this: 'We must teach methods of interpretation if we claim to teach history. . . . We cannot leave the teaching of historical method to incidental learning while we concentrate in class upon amassing factual information.'[25]

We have already seen how reluctant professional historians were to press too hard the case against amassing factual information. The young history teacher in the classroom is conscious of dangers every whit as grave as historical relativism when he seeks to break out of the straitjacket of historical facts. First, most examination papers have changed little since the days of Ince. Mrs Lawrence has shown how textbooks in schools have sustained, and been sustained by, these same examinations. In his beginnings, the young history teacher then is at once confronted with strong external pressure to provide factual information for his pupils, and to be judged by their success in absorbing the material. Second, he has a sneaking suspicion that imaginative work is easier than the 'hard facts': the Hearnshaw view of the imagination as a holiday from the facts dies hard. This lie must be nailed. Our standards should be *more*, not *less*, austere for the evaluation of children's imaginative work. We must insist, with Collingwood, that it be rooted in evidence. To take a small example. A pupil in a junior form in a secondary school is asked to imagine that he is a monk imprisoned by Henry VIII. He is to write a letter to Rome, explaining his plight. Fine writing is not enough. This is an historical, not literary, exercise. He must substantiate his arguments with evidence. But where will the average pupil obtain it? He will want to know what it was like to be a monk in Tudor times: what kind of food would you eat? where would you live? what would you do for the poor? what would you believe in? It is safe to say that he would have obtained very few of these answers from a textbook as 'factual' as Ince's *Outlines of English History*. If too many of our textbooks are still reincarnations of Ince, something of value may nevertheless be teased out of them. And this is the worth of imaginative work, such as the Tudor monk's letter: it forces the asking of the right questions. Even if the textbook is inadequate—and, mercifully, a good textbook series such as Longman's *Then and There* is becoming less rare in the classroom—and let us suppose that it only contained a drab outline of the main political events in Henry VIII's reign, these events themselves take on a new dimension when seen through the eyes of a defeated opponent. The Fall of Wolsey, the Reformation Parliament, the Dissolution of the Monasteries—these become, not facts to be learned, but experiences to be lived through. The professional historian is the pupil writ large. He, too, has to make unpromising material, like Pipe Rolls, yield information by asking the right questions. He, too, has to construct a coherent picture from fragmentary material. The professional historian has to deal with immensely complex questions, such as the critical evaluation of sources. But this is a difference of degree, not of kind. One cannot say the same of the more 'factual' approach: 'Read pages 83-97 of your textbook, in preparation for a test on the reign of Henry VIII.' One approach—however humble and groping—is on the path that leads to the writing of history; the other—however sincere and well-intentioned—is on the path that leads to victory in television quiz programmes.

The two approaches are strikingly affirmed in one pupil's exercise book.[26] An eleven-year-old who changed schools moved from a conventional teaching of history to one where a student-teacher had totally different aspirations for his pupils. On the same page of the pupil's exercise book appeared two different historical exercises. One was as follows:

Houses in Georgian Days

Great houses such as Buckingham House, and Blenheim Palace were built with a splendid central block to which the kitchens on the one hand and the stables on the other were connected by a collonade. In the high classed houses the ceilings were covered with plaster designs and pictures, usually in the Italian style. Robert Adam, a popular architect of this time, designed many of the lofty drawing-rooms in these great houses in his own style. Many of his rooms had curved ceilings, and plaster decorations in delicate shades of pink, green and blue. Georgian houses of moderate size were perhaps the most pleasant looking houses built. The outside of the houses was usually plain and simple, of red brick or white stucco. The roof was tiled and had dormer windows, but no gables.

The second item was:

Inverness Press: April 17th 1746

1000 SOLDIERS KILLED

On the 16th April 1746 the battle of Culloden between Bonnie Prince Charles and Cumberland. The defeat of Cumberland over 600 horses being found dead. Cumberland was seen by soldiers riding of and disappearing. More news in the *Inverness Express*. A Highlander named Macdonald spoke to reporters about the battle. He just said that as long as the Highlanders won he was pleased.

This is not a loaded antithesis: a brilliant piece of imaginative writing set against a banal factual account. Rather, the antithesis is loaded the other way. The first extract is work produced by an enlightened teacher, who knew that there was more to history than Reform Bills and Conventicle Acts. The second extract is poor stuff. The student-teacher may have been too inexperienced to involve the class; the pupil may have been bewildered by the change of style demanded of him. Housman remarked that 'accuracy is a duty, not a virtue'. So out-of-touch was the *Inverness Press* that its reporter assumed that Cumberland had *lost* Culloden! In this case the teacher could immediately recall the pupil to his duty; the imaginative work had exposed the depths of misunderstanding. Misunderstandings, on the other hand, could be concealed, in the first extract, beneath the smooth surface of the teacher's (or textbook's) mandarin prose. Accuracy had been made *the* virtue; the price was the loss of any personal involvement by the pupil. And that is why the second extract, for all its defects, has intimations which the first extract, for all its virtues, could never share.

If the young history teacher remains nervous about the transfer from Georgian houses to the *Inverness Press* it may be for one very good reason. He may simply be repelled by the *modishness* of claims for the *mode of inquiry*. To argue that the author of the *Inverness Press* is behaving like G. R. Elton will offend more people than G. R. Elton: the whole world of Bruner, Bloom's taxonomies, Collingwood and Carr seems absurdly alien from the realities of 4Z on a Friday afternoon. The pomposity and imprecision of claims put forward for pupils to simulate the historian's mode of inquiry has frequently repelled the young teacher. Edwin Fenton's *Teaching the New Social Studies in Secondary Schools* is, I believe, an important argument for relating the activities of the history pupil to those of the professional historian. But some of its more strident claims need to be tempered; and have been—gently but decisively—by M. M. Krug.[28] As Krug points out, the idea of a *whole curriculum* based on the inductive method is *not* a very practical possibility; nor even a very desirable one. There is a time—perhaps even as rarely as once a year—when pupils should be given the 'Fenton' challenge: be asked to respond to original documents and to display such skills as detection of bias, sifting of evidence, comparison of authorities and the suchlike. There are other times when the history teacher will simply tell his pupils a good story.

Yet, in a less specialised way than Fenton has argued, we should retain his insight that the historian's mode of inquiry *is* at the heart of our subject. In a recent article, Gareth Jones argued that the study of history should, *at any stage*, enshrine four principles:[29]

(1) Historians study history because they want to enjoy it and because they want to find out what happened in the past.
(2) They tend to work on problems and not periods.
(3) In their research they are working on their own, tackling problems at first-hand, though naturally with guide-lines from the existing store of knowledge.
(4) They are getting down to the grass roots by studying the raw material of history, documents as well as other types of sources, and attempting to interpret them.

This is pedestrian—trite even—and historians and history teachers will quarrel with the wording. I still welcome the statement for three reasons. It is not pompous. On these criteria, teachers need not, and should not, feel immodest in claiming to develop historical skills in their pupils. It justifies the subject in terms of skills, rather than content matter; recognising the truth of Professor Galbraith's aphorism that 'the study of history is a personal matter, in which the activity is generally more valuable than the result'.[30] Finally, it underlines the truth that pupils do not need to engage in (4) all the time, in the Fenton sense, in order to imitate the historian's craft; in (1), (2) and (3) they can be engaged in 'imaginative re-creation'—although at a different *level* from that of the historian.

And yet if we leave our aims in history teaching at Gareth Jones's level of generality we may have made an illusory advance upon the aims put forward at the beginning of this chapter by 'Mr Black', 'Miss Denton', 'Mr Freeman' and 'Miss Spender'. 'Old Luther' will never be slain until we have moved beyond these useful generalities, isolated the skills we want to cultivate in our pupils, and then related these skills to the actual examination papers which the pupils take. The most hopeful sign for our beginners in history teaching is that these changes are happening. When Pat and Chris describe, in their chapters, the very careful ways in which they are trying to introduce their pupils to the historian's craft, it is striking how unperturbed they are by the notion that 'the reformation has to come in'. In their concern to assess their pupils' historical skills they are receiving growing support from educational research: two recent Historical Association pamphlets, *The Development of Thinking and The Learning of History*, and *Educational Objectives for the Study of History*, by Jeanette B. Coltham (the latter in collaboration with

John Fines), take us well beyond Jones's generalities although still in harmony with the principles that he outlined; the Schools Council Examination Bulletin No. 18, *The Certificate of Secondary Education: The Place of the Personal Topic—History,* offers some useful practical hints on how to isolate historical skills for that particular examination; Mr Derek Turner and Mr James Mason of Christ's Hospital, Horsham, will shortly be publishing an interesting paper which shows how their whole school syllabus and culminating fifth-year examination will be related to skills, not content. The exchange between Jones and his teacher, which is quoted as the epigraph to this volume, prompted George Orwell to ask: 'Is that kind of thing still going on, I wonder?' The humour of the exchange lay in the fragility of memory as a basis for historical understanding: for Jones, the French Revolution might just as well have been caused by the people's oppression of the nobility as the other way round. But the real obscenity lies at a deeper level. Even if Jones had not blundered, what is exceptionable about the exchange is the assumption that the French Revolution *had* three causes. If the pupil gives two, he is inadequate; if he gives four, he is arrogant. This authoritarianism accords ill with the historian's craft—as Elton and Carr no less than Collingwood have defined it—and it is the historian's world of guesses, hypotheses, fumblings and conjectures that Pat and Chris are trying to capture in their work with young pupils.

Haltingly, newer examination papers are recognising this truth. Not, as in the C.S.E. East Midlands Region paper of 1965, when they ask pupils a question like this:

> Imagine yourself living at the end of the seventeenth century.
> (*a*) Explain why the Protestants disliked James II.
> (*b*) Describe how William and Mary came to the throne.
> (*c*) Show how Parliament increased its power 1688-1701.

This is Ince flesh tarted up in Collingwood clothes. But a year later, from another C.S.E. Board (Associated Lancashire), we get this splendid question, legitimately calling upon pupils to respond to evidence:

> Read the following extract which was written by a French Clergyman, the Abbé Provost, during a stay he made in England in the 1730's:
>
>> 'I have had pointed out to me in several coffee-houses a couple of lords, a baronet, a showmaker, a tailor, a wine-merchant and some others of the same sort, all sitting round the same table and discussing familiarly the views of

the court and of the town. The government's affairs are as much the concern of the people as of the great. Every man has a right to discuss them freely. Men condemn, approve, revile, with bitter invectives, both in speech and writing without the authorities daring to intervene. The King himself is not secure from censure. The coffee-houses and other public places are the seats of English liberty. For two pence you have the right to read all the papers for and against the government and to take a cup of tea or coffee as well.'

(a) Explain in a couple of lines what a coffee-house was.
(b) Lloyd's coffee-house became exceptionally well known because people with certain interests met there—what interests?
(c) The Abbé lists the people he has seen in a coffee-house. Why do you think this list seemed remarkable in his eyes?
(d) What does the following mean: 'The King himself is not secure from censure'?
(e) In about four lines explain why these coffee-houses were 'the seats of English liberty'.

There are other encouraging parallel developments. The C.S.E. Personal Topic has shown how well unacademic pupils respond to the challenge of producing original work of their own.[31] The same has been true, for a longer period of time, with students at many Colleges of Education: their special studies, produced over two years, are the only form of history examining which I actually look forward to reading in the summer. And it is historians' *questions* that the recent Schools Council paper expects to be the contribution of history to humanities programmes—'*how* do we know? what is the *source* of our information, *to what extent* may it be relied upon?'—not, as in the days of the old Social Studies programmes, historians' *answers*.[32]

John Berger's brilliant study of a country doctor was entitled *A Fortunate Man*. In a fascinating way the experiences of Sassall, Berger's hero, overlap with the experiences of the teacher/beginners. Pat, Carlos and Chris are fortunate too. They have a skill; they care for their subject; they care what their subject should be doing for their children. During their year of training, they learned their craft working alongside a master: John Townsend. They learned about the problems of school organisation, and the challenges to it posed by a new humanities programme, with Peter Mitchell. With Colin Brent, they learned the hazards as well as the rewards in compiling archive kits. From Frances Lawrence, they understood the menace posed by the school textbook. They knew, before they began full-time teaching, that the challenge they faced was to convert history, in the minds of their pupils, from a joyless rote-learning drudgery into a meaningful and joyful activity. They were gaining a sense of mastery.

That sense of mastery was not entirely lost in their beginnings as teachers. But during the first few months—and for perhaps longer —that sense was swamped by a more powerful sense of *masterlessness*. Pat's new school was so strikingly different—in its virtues as well as its defects—from Thomas Bennett, that this change is perhaps most marked in her account. Yet even when the schools were less different, the change was also there; arguably, if the school were an identical twin of Thomas Bennett, the change would still be there. For, even if the building and organisation were the same, the children would not be. It is facile to say that, in their beginnings, Pat, Carlos and Chris have moved from a subject-centred approach to a child-centred approach. Facile and wrong. In their training year, they were already sensitive to the responses of their pupils. In their beginnings as history teachers they would continue to nag away at the problems posed in shifting the emphasis of their subject from *content* to *mode of inquiry*. But for the young teacher, as for the country doctor, dominant obsessions have changed. As Berger put it:

> Previously the sense of mastery which Sassall gained was the result of the skill with which he dealt with emergencies. The possible complications would all appear to develop within his own field: they were medical complications. He remained the central character. Now the patient is the central character. He tries to recognise each patient and, having recognised him, he tries to set an example for him—not a morally improving example, but an example wherein the patient can recognise himself.

Carlos's contacts with his pupils on the football field, Dick's outing on the school bus with Neil, Alan and Graham, are to be seen not as nervous, ingratiating gestures nor yet as a substitute for reflecting about their subject. They are, rather, the recognition that this contact is the essential preliminary to advances within the classroom; the contact which Sassall achieves in physical activity alongside the villagers:

> The area in which Sassall practises is one of extreme cultural

deprivation, even by British standards. And it was only by working with many of the men of the village and coming to understand something of their techniques that he could qualify for their conversation. They then came to share a language which was a metaphor for the rest of their common experience.[33]

Pat, Carlos and Chris are coming to share a language with their pupils: they are at their beginnings.

NOTES

[1] L. B. Stone, *The Crisis of the Aristocracy 1558-1641* (Oxford University Press, 1961), p. 680.

[2] Incorporated Association of Assistant Masters in Secondary Schools, *The Teaching of History in Secondary Schools* (Cambridge University Press, 1965), pp. 2-3.

[3] Martin Booth, *History Betrayed?* (Longman's Curriculum Reform Series, 1969), pp. 57, 61.

[4] Mary Price, 'History in Danger', *History*, 1968, pp. 342-47.

[5] Booth, op. cit., p. 17.

[6] E. H. Carr, *What is History?* (Pelican, 1964), p. 23.

[7] G. Talbot Griffith, 'The Correlation of School and University Teaching: A Discussion', *History*, 1929, pp. 33-42.

[8] M. V. C. Jeffreys, *History in Schools* (Pitman, 1948), p. 46.

[9] Carr, op. cit., p. 21. Mr George Grieve, Principal Lecturer in History at Moray House College of Education, Edinburgh, has been the pioneer in drawing out the implications of Collingwood's thought in the field of classroom history.

[10] G. R. Elton, *The Practice of History* (Fontana, 1969), pp. 75-79.

[11] Ibid., p. 85.

[12] Carr, op. cit., pp. 25-29.

[13] R. G. Collingwood, *The Idea of History* (Oxford Paperbacks, 1961), p. 246.

[14] Christopher Blake, 'Can History Be Objective?', *Theories of History*, ed. Patrick Gardiner (New York, 1965), pp. 329-44.

[15] Elton, op. cit., p. 79. J. G. A. Pocock's essay, 'Working on Ideas in Time', will appear in a collection of his essays, *Politics, Language and Time*, shortly to be published by the Atheneum Press. Pocock analyses *his* history in terms of *his* philosophy: the result, to my mind, is the best description by a working historian of his mode of inquiry; encouragingly akin to the skills that Pat, Carlos and Chris are seeking to foster in their pupils.

[16] Ibid., pp. 112, 78, 187, 200.

[17] Collingwood, op. cit., pp. 265-66.

[18] Norman Mailer, *The Idol and the Octopus* (New York, 1968), p. 73.

[19] Another example of what Collingwood did *not* mean by use of the imagination: Professor Peel (*Studies in the Nature and Teaching of History*, ed., W. Burston and D. Thompson, London, 1967, p. 184) quotes from one R. Symm-Crampton: 'History can also be a great stimulus to the imagination. It should never be the mere compilation of bare facts. *We fill in the gaps* by using imagination and intuition.' My italics.

[20] Collingwood, op. cit., p. 305. This is an instance where it is equally as unblessed to receive as to give. Collingwood was sorry for the historian; making really the same point, the Schools Council Working Paper No. 11, *Society and the Young School Leaver*, p. 3, was sorry for those at the receiving end: 'A frequent cause of failure seems to be that the course is often based on the traditional belief that there is a body of content for each separate subject which every young school leaver should know.'

[21] H. R. Trevor-Roper, *The Rise of Christian Europe* (London, 1965), p. 9.

[22] Not so fanciful as it sounds. I have recently been concerned with preparing a new type of 'A' level history paper that would test judgement, not memory. The board have now asked me to draw up a set of Model Answers.

[23] Schools Council Report, *Humanities for the Young School Leaver. An Approach Through History* (Evans/Methuen Educational, 1969), p. 15.

[24] Sybil Marshall, *Adventure in Creative Education* (Pergamon, 1968).

[25] Edwin Fenton, *Teaching the New Social Studies in Secondary Schools* (New York, 1966), p. 150. See William R. Taylor, 'A Laboratory Course in American History', *Journal of Higher Education*, XXXIX, 9, 1968, pp. 497-505, for an interesting application of Fenton's ideals to university teaching.

[26] My former colleague, Mr John Thwaites, Senior Lecturer in History at Aberdeen College of Education, spotted the significance of this 'Jekyll and Hyde' phenomenon when supervising the teaching practice of one of his students.

[27] Carr, op. cit., p. 10.

[28] M. M. Krug, *History and the Social Sciences* (Blaisdell, 1967).

[29] Gareth E. Jones, 'Towards a Theory of History Teaching', *History*, 1970, pp. 54-64.

[30] Arthur Marwick, *The Nature of History* (Macmillan, 1970), p. 245.

[31] *The Certificate of Secondary Education: The Place of the Personal Topic—History* (Schools Council Examinations Bulletin, No. 18, 1968).

[32] *Humanities for the Young School Leaver . . .*, p. 19.

[33] John Berger, *A Fortunate Man* (Penguin, 1969), pp. 77, 100.

5

HISTORY IN HUMANITIES PROGRAMMES

SINCE Peter Mitchell's essay on Humanities Programmes was written, one year of Thomas Bennett Fifth Formers has already taken 'O' level or C.S.E. in Humanities (history, geography and social science), and very soon a second year will have been completed. It is possible to make some interim judgements on how far initial hopes have been fulfilled. Geography and social science lie outside the concern of this volume but it is clear that historians feel misgivings about the contribution that history is at present making to the integrated programme. John Townsend, as Head of the History Department, and Colin Brent and myself (who are taking turns to be the History External Moderator) can now see, with hindsight, some points where we went wrong. Our experience may be useful for other history teachers who want to contribute to Humanities Programmes.

Historians are reluctant to see their discipline participate in such programmes often because the proposed offer of union is a concealed rape. History becomes a milch-cow for sociological hypotheses. When this is done well—as in Michael Walzer's audacious attempt to see puritanism as a 'modernising' ideology (*The Revolution of the Saints*, Weidenfeld and Nicolson, 1966)—the result is often arresting without even then allaying legitimate reservations by historians (see C. H. George's *critique* of Walzer in *Past and Present*, 41, pp. 77-104). When it is done less well the historians' discomfort is proportionately greater.

It is important to realise that, contrariwise, the magnet for historians of the Thomas Bennett Humanities Programme was that the offer of union was not spurious: history was asked to make its contribution *in its own right*, and not as a useful storehouse of background information. This is clear in the original course objectives for history in the programme, which were as follows:

(*a*) To foster an interest in the past and by a developing time sense to discover its relevance to the present;

(*b*) To understand the historical basis of the student's physical environment;

M   177

(c) To develop skills in the collecting (with special reference to original sources), and the evaluating, of materials to establish the truth about the past;

(d) To be cautious about accepting generalisations about the past and to be ready to test them by reference to facts;

(e) To appreciate the reality and uniqueness of each historical person, event and period by close study of selected patches.

There may be objections to each one of these course objectives except the most telling: it was not imposed from above, but arose as a consensus from lengthy discussions among the Thomas Bennett teachers themselves. What then went wrong?

Two things, I would suggest. One was that the five skills were isolated *explicitly* in the course objectives, but only *implicitly* in the course outline, which was defined in terms of content. The students would study, for instance, the extension of the English franchise in their fourth year and themes such as 'Nationalism' and 'War' in the fifth. To these topics they *would be expected* to bring those skills which were outlined in the course objectives. Why not try to have your cake and eat it?

There is something attractive, to all of us who want our pupils to be mature, informed citizens, in the idea of combining the exercise of relevant discipline skills with the acquisition of information about the world today. The task is not impossible, but its difficulties should not be underrated, as they were in this case. The snare is this: the more attractive the available material, and the more powerfully relevant the topic to present-day concerns, the more easy it is to slide from achieving the content objectives into assuming that the skills objectives have been similarly mastered. Students know this from their ordinary history lessons: without the most diligent self-consciousness about what skills they hope their pupils will cultivate in each given lesson, content will irresistibly take over the task from them. And—whatever the lofty long-term aims of the students—in practice the aim of the lesson will be to complete the work on Gladstone's Second Ministry which had been begun in the previous lesson!

The aim—that pupils should imitate the *mode of inquiry* of the historian—is likely, it seems to me, to remain a pious shibboleth unless the syllabus content is built *explicitly* around these criteria. This is the position that Derek Turner and James Mason, of Christ's Hospital, Horsham, have adopted with their Mode 3 'O' Level History Paper, to which I refer in the fourth section of the book. The consequences of such a radical position must also be faced: that in searching for the material that can call upon the teacher's own specialist skills and enthusiasm, and which he feels confident can afford the same scope for his pupils, he may be led in directions from a content point of view which seem to marry ill with the interests of other parts of the Humanities Programme. For example, the first topic for the Christ's Hospital fourth-year course is a reconstruction of the story of two eleventh-century queens, Emma and Aelgifu. If the history teacher feels that he can cultivate the pupils' historical skills in an area closer to the interests of geographer and social scientist than that provided by Emma and Aelgifu— and there is no inherent reason why he should not feel this—with the same confidence that Mr Turner invests in Emma and Aelgifu, union is possible; if not, not.

The second mistake was closely related to the first. Skills objectives became swallowed up by content objectives: that was the first wrong turning. The second wrong turning was the failure to recognise how closely the first four skills objectives were dependent upon the fulfilment of the fifth. As far as I know there was no hierarchy of objectives: the last was not intended to be the least. But the fifth objective—'to appreciate the reality and uniqueness of each historical person, event and period by close study of selected patches'—has a modest air beside the first four. In retrospect the failure to fulfil the fifth objective can now be seen as crucial.

What are the virtues of a 'patch' study? They give children *time* to soak themselves in one small area, familiarise themselves with source materials, cultivate skills in handling documents, explore areas other than the political (such as cultural, social, religious, intellectual, economic), and acquire mastery of this small field. These are considerable virtues in any history syllabus, but they are not the only virtues. A good case can be made for studying history through topics: the 'Line of Development' approach argued so cogently by M. V. C. Jeffreys in his two articles in *History* in, respectively, 1935 (pp. 233-42) and 1936 (pp. 230-38).

My experience with the Thomas Bennett Humanities Programme has, however, led me to a conclusion which I had not anticipated: that only in a 'patch' study, and a series of related 'patch' studies, can history enter into a Humanities Programme with its integrity secure. It seems to me that the virtues of a 'Line of Development' syllabus—its sweep; its boldness in pursuing one theme and jettisoning those themes which are irrelevant to its pursuit even if they are contemporary with it; its ease in relating to present-day concerns—are virtues which are already there *in the commitment to a Humanities Programme*. One of the historical themes of the Thomas Bennett Fourth Year is 'The Extension of the Franchise': this is a legitimate historical 'Line of Development' theme. It relates well to later fifth-year themes, such as 'Democracy in Britain', 'War' and 'Marxism', but at a price. The price enacted becomes clear when one sees the scripts of the pupils themselves: where the complexity of English political development—its residual conservatism even—is obscured by a modern 'Whiggery' broadening out from Reform Bills to Dock Strikes. I feel that a fourth-year 'patch' on Late Victorian England would have provided the missing dimension and indeed a securer base for fifth-year explorations. To put it in a grander way: the 'patch' study provides a corrective 'idiographic' element, that is, it particularises; the 'Line of Development' themes reinforce the 'nomothetic' element—the design to establish general laws—which is at the heart of the contribution which the social sciences are already making to other areas of the Humanities Programme. The argument, it will be seen, is not then the familiar one that too much history content is being squeezed out by Humanities Programmes, nor even that there is anything improper in the study of history in the context of areas of interest that impinge on those of the geographer and social scientist. I would argue the contrary: that history can be only the beneficiary of such experiments, always provided that the contribution which it makes *as a discipline* is vitally different from, and not a pale replica of, the other disciplines within that programme. The paradox is this: the true assertion of the discipline may mean *less*, not *more*, history content within a Humanities Programme. Pupils in their fourth year who find the *time* to learn historical skills, to become familiar with the sources, to appreciate the complexity of events, which is possible in a 'patch' study of Late Victorian England would perhaps be in a more informed position to understand 'Democracy in Britain Today' in their fifth year. This conviction is shaping our rethinking that is now going on about the contribution of history to the Humanities Programme.

This then is not the story of rape disguised as courtship. On the contrary: the maiden was wooed and won over a long period of time; the vows to respect her integrity were sincere and binding. If the maiden has cause for complaint it is that the honeymoon ardour was excessive: she was asked to yield too quickly what could only be yielded over a longer period of time. The result was premature ejaculation on the one side and a sense of deprivation on the other. The moral is not that such unions are doomed to failure —back to spinsterhood!—but that the virtues of slowness and patience can never be emphasised enough.

SUGGESTIONS FOR FURTHER READING

HISTORY as a school subject dates effectively from the establishment of the School of Modern History at Oxford in 1872 and the Historical Tripos at Cambridge in 1874. Thus was the pattern set: the decisive influence on the teaching of history came from the Universities *downwards*. The challenge to the subject has come from the opposite direction: from the primary school *upwards*. The response of subject teachers has, in general, not been a very dignified one: caught with their pants down, they have scuttled in terror to their subject latrines. And in the heat of child-centred *v.* subject-centred controversies, hardly anybody noticed that it was a very antiquated (*c.* 1872-74) concept of subject that was being discussed. Historians think very differently now about their subject from what their predecessors did (admittedly 'O' level examinations would suggest the opposite). This is where history compares unfavourably with, say, English: there is nobody quite like David Holbrook, bridging the gap between education and subject.

Two consequences of this: (1) the student will have to do a lot of work himself in attempting to correlate changing views about the subject with changing views about education; (2) an awful lot of books on the teaching of history are still rooted in Victorian preconceptions about the subject (a few of them are actually written in Victorian times) and can be ignored. What then is left?

The student should begin by possessing *The Teaching of History*, issued by the Incorporated Association of Assistant Masters in Secondary Schools (Cambridge University Press). This is the third edition and is radically different from the earlier two: although tinged with the cowardice of committees, it is a very useful book. *Teaching History* (Ministry of Education Pamphlet No. 23), is less comprehensive but good, in an urbane sort of way. There are some thoughtful essays in: *Studies in the Nature and Teaching of History*, ed. W. H. Burston and D. Thompson (Routledge and Kegan Paul). E. M. Lewis, *Teaching History in Secondary Schools* (Evans), is sensible. F. C. Happold, *The Approach to History* (Chatto and Windus), has worn well: the student may dig some valuable insights out of it.

Marjorie Hourd, *The Education of the Poetic Spirit* (Heinemann), is not ostensibly about the teaching of history at all. Don't be fooled by that: there is more of value in this classic than in a hundred ordinary manuals on the teaching of history. The title is the only off-putting thing in the book.

There has not been nearly enough critical thinking about changes in the concept of the subject. Thus last-ditch defenders of traditional 'O' level and 'A' level syllabuses have been able to get away with the pose of being defenders of the interests of their *subject*. Unfortunately child-centred critics have tacitly conceded them this point; perhaps this is why the effect of the well-meaning, but intellectually low-powered, bromides on the teaching of history in the Plowden and Newsom Reports has been so curiously muffled (the section on the teaching of history in the Scottish Education Department Report, 1955, *Junior Secondary Education*, has more punch than its English counterparts). The more telling criticism of subject 'orthodoxies' is that they are a prostitution of the subject *itself*.

This is the point raised obliquely in E. H. Carr, *What is History?* (Pelican). The first chapter, 'The Historian and His Facts', most entertainingly emphasises the differences between modern historians and their Victorian predecessors. Carr acknowledges freely his debt to R. G. Collingwood, *The Idea of History* (Oxford). Collingwood is very difficult to read, very easy to caricature (Carr does this himself in the first chapter). But his influence on the professional historian has been immense. It will be interesting to see, in the next generation, whether his influence on the history teacher will be equally marked. A useful general guide to philosophies of history is *Theories of History*, ed. P. Gardiner (Allen and Unwin). Especially good is the contribution of Christopher Blake, 'Can History be Objective?'

Some robust blows for a wider historical syllabus than our conventional insular framework allows have been struck by G. Barraclough, *History in a Changing World* (Blackwell), and his provocative 'Presidential Address to the Historical Association', *History and the Common Man*, in April, 1966. Less shrill, and perhaps more persuasive, is the recent important Education Pamphlet 52, *Towards World History* (H.M.S.O.). E. H. Dance, *History the Betrayer* (Hutchinson), has written usefully on the problems of historical bias. M. Bloch, *The Historian's Craft* (Manchester U.P.); H. Butterfield, *The Whig Interpretation of History* (Bell); I. Berlin, *The Hedgehog and the Fox* (Weidenfeld and Nicolson): three different approaches to the problem of writing history, but equally stimulating. There is also A. L. Rowse's brash little book, *The Use of History* (English University Press).

M. V. C. Jeffreys is the pioneer of the 'line of development' history syllabus. Therefore his *History in Schools* (Pitman) must be read, although some of his assumptions may seem less tenable now than when they were first written. There is no apologist for the 'patch' approach, which has been the other significant alternative to the old-fashioned chronological syllabus that has become popular in recent years. The nearest to it is: P. Carpenter, *History Teaching: The Era Approach* (Cambridge), rather defensive, but pleasantly undogmatic. Perhaps the best insight to the 'patch' approach is given by looking at one of the best textbooks in the admirable *Then and There Series* (Longman), *The Medieval Village* by Marjorie Reeves. The series was originally aimed at the older children in the primary school. It has been a powerful force for good in the lower forms of many secondary schools, and shows the value of having a scholar who cares about her subject *and* pupils writing for the junior forms.

Sheila Ferguson, *Projects in History* (Batsford), has been written very much with an eye on current developments in the C.S.E. history syllabuses: it would be a valuable book for the student to buy. *The Jackdaws* (Cape), have been an exciting but ambivalent development in the 'project' field. The posters in *History Class Pictures* (Macmillan) are of great value to the history student; if they are too expensive, there are small reproductions of them in *History Picture Books* (Macmillan). An interesting series is: 'The University of Sheffield Institute of Education Local History Pamphlets', under the general editorship of Gordon Batho, and obtainable from the Sheffield University Institute of Education. The series, *They Saw it Happen* (Blackwell), if handled properly, can transform many history lessons. *A History of Everyday Things in England*, ed. C. M. B. and M. Quennell (Batsford), is a very useful book for the teacher to have beside him for reference. Historical novels are a source that have been under-employed in the teaching of history at schools: see Helen Cam, *Historical Novels* (Historical Association Pamphlet, G.48) and a useful list in Ferguson, *op. cit.*, pp. 118-28. The Schools Council Working Paper No. 11, *Society and the Young School Leaver*, argues powerfully the need for us all to think critically about the traditional subject curriculum.

Jerome Bruner, *The Process of Education* (Harvard U.P.), has been the most original critic of traditional concepts of what a curriculum should be. His influence has been decisive on the 'new' maths and physics. What about the 'new' history? Edwin Fenton, in an important book, *Teaching the New Social Studies in Secondary Schools:*

An Inductive Approach (Holt, Rinehart & Winston), argues that we *can* 'Brunerize' history. The archive kits that are being produced in the United States in response to these developments have their parallel in work being produced at Universities here (notably Sheffield, Nottingham, Newcastle, Birmingham and Sussex). Ultimately there will need to be a central bank of such material for teachers to draw on. Meanwhile a first instalment from Newcastle, *Coals from Newcastle* (Newcastle-upon-Tyne Archive Teaching Units, No. 1), shows how far such work is soaring *beyond* Jackdaws. Sybil Marshall in her two books, *An Experiment in Education*, and *Adventure in Creative Education* (Pergamon), shows how relevant the techniques of the primary school are to secondary school history. And the Schools Council Examinations Bulletin No. 18, *The Certificate of Secondary Education: The Place of the Personal Topic — History* (H.M.S.O.), shows the beneficial effects on history teaching in schools when examinations are devised that make intelligent allowance for all these recent developments. The millennium is a long way off, but at least we are beginning to move beyond 1872! That is the most hopeful conclusion to draw from the important collection of essays, *New Movements in the Study and Teaching of History*, ed. M. Ballard (Maurice Temple Smith). Moreover, the situation is not entirely hopeless for the young history teacher when a new journal can be produced which is so down-to-earth and helpful as *Teaching History* (Historical Association).

The most valuable bibliographical source on the teaching of history is John Fines's witty and epigrammatic *The Teaching of History in the United Kingdom* (Historical Association Helps for Students of History, No. 77, 1969). Fines is hopeful but not complacent: 'People are writing and talking about history teaching as never before. We are on the crest of a wave.' Something of the advance in writing about history can be measured by comparing the 1972 edition of W. H. Burston and C. W. Green, *Handbook for History Teachers* (Methuen), with the much inferior first edition of 1962. But it is disturbing that the Editors should have included the essay by P. C. Gasson and W. P. Stokes on 'G.C.E. (Ordinary Level) and C.S.E. Examinations'—'all the questions are—or should be—unambiguous, and in most instances there is only one answer' (*ibid.*, p. 175)—alongside thoughtful contributions from scholars like Donald Thompson, Anthony Edwards and Margaret Bryant (all of which repay a close study).

Among the recent books that have contributed to the new climate must be named: Martin Booth, *History Betrayed?* (Longmans, 1969); W. H. Burston, *Principles of History Teaching* (Methuen, 1972);

J. Fines, *History* (Blond, 1969); J. A. Fairley, *Patch History and Creativity* (Longmans, 1970); A. Jamieson, *Practical History Teaching* (Evans, 1971); M. M. Krug, *History and the Social Sciences* (Blaisdell, 1967). John Fines has brought his bibliography on teaching history up to date with an *Addendum* in *Teaching History*, 1971, II, 6, pp. 153-157. Joy Hancock and Helen Johnson ('Archive Kits in the Secondary School', *Teaching History*, 1972, 11, 7, pp. 207-217) describe their experience, while they were students on our course, of producing Archive Kits on *Rottingdean Village* and *Turnpike Roads in Sussex 1750-1850*, respectively: thus interestingly complementing Colin Brent's essay in this volume (pp. 93-110). Another Sussex researcher, David Gee, has examined the assumptions behind Sixth Form teaching of our subject in a number of different countries (*History at 18*, University of Sussex D. Phil.Thesis, 1972, Unpublished). This volume has dedicated itself to two propositions: that the history pupil's quarry should be the mode of inquiry of the historian; that this is an extremely difficult and complex task in practice. Research that stresses the second point is welcome—the demonstration by Peel (Burston and Thompson, *op. cit.*, pp. 159-191) and Hallam (Ballard, *op cit.*, pp. 162-179) of children's difficulties with formal, operational concepts; the chastening results of the political vocabulary test with Sixth Formers (I. Lister, ed., *Bulletin of General Studies Association*, 1968, no. 12., pp. 36-39); Professor G. R. Elton's analysis of the complexity of the historian's skills in his *The Practice of History* (Fontana), as part of his belief that 'documents thrown naked before the untrained mind turn from pearls to paste'—always provided that it is not abused to stress the *impossibility* (as opposed to the *difficulty*) of achieving the first point. Jeanette Coltham, *The Development of Thinking and the Learning of History* (Historical Association Pamphlet, 1971), pp. 34-35, strikes the right balance in her assertion that in a *teaching* as opposed to a *testing* situation (as Hallam's work, for example, was), the moral to be drawn by the teacher from Hallam's researches is not to under-rate the care that is required when the occasion demands it in lowering the conceptual level from the formal to the concrete to assist the pupils' understanding, rather than to abandon altogether the attempt to teach history as a rational study for young minds. Dr Coltham's promise (*Teaching History*, 1972, 11, 7, pp. 278-279) in future issues of that journal to apply her framework of educational objectives to 'O' Level syllabuses, Teaching Units and documentary material is one of the heartening signs of future advance in the teaching of our subject.

W. M. L.

NOTES ON CONTRIBUTORS

JOHN TOWNSEND is Head of History Department, Thomas Bennett Comprehensive School, Crawley, Sussex.

MRS PAT KENDELL is a graduate of Keele, now teaching in a secondary school.

CARLOS HOOD is a graduate of York, now teaching in a secondary school.

CHRIS CULPIN is a graduate of Cambridge, now teaching in a secondary school.

COLIN BRENT is Lecturer in History at Brighton College of Education.

MRS FRANCES LAWRENCE is research student at the University of Sussex.

PETER MITCHELL is Head of Humanities at Thomas Bennett Comprehensive School, Crawley.

WILLIAM LAMONT is Reader in History and Education at the University of Sussex.

INDEX